Practical Chinese™

實用中文™

讀、說、寫

The Effective Way of Learning Reading, Writing, and Speaking Chinese
(Traditional Characters)

第四冊

LEVEL 4

王姚文編寫　　(by Wendy Lin)

版權所有　　不准翻印

Copyright © 2005
CREATIVE WORLD ENT., INC.
43 Candlewick Court, Matawan, New Jersey 07747
Practicalchinese@gmail.com
www.practicalchinese.com
(732) 441-1704

Introduction

"Practical Chinese", also known as "The Effective Way of Learning Reading, Writing, and Speaking Chinese", is a series of ten books from the beginner level to the advanced level and is especially designed for native English speakers. The first two books, "For Beginner I" and "For Beginner II", provide various activities to make learning fun and easy and do not have writing drills. The context of Level I through Level IV focus on daily conversation. Level V through Level VIII is related to the Chinese culture and histories, which allow the readers to learn the language as well as the culture. In addition, the book "Chinese for Children" is a coloring and activity book for the preschool learners.

The vocabulary used in each chapter context gradually builds up from the previous chapters. In order to help the learners study independently, pinyin has been used through out the books other than the various exercises provided in each chapter. Pinyin is a Chinese word that means using the English alphabet to spell the sounds of Chinese characters. Details about pinyin can be found in Level 1 of the series.

The entire book series include the following books:

For Beginner I   Fun Way of learning reading, and speaking Chinese
For Beginner II   Fun Way of learning reading, and speaking Chinese
Level 1   My family, my friends, my schools, and myself….
Level II   Self introduction
Level III   Interests, occupations, animals………..
Level IV   Daily conversation
Level V   Introduction of Chinese festivals
Level VI   Introduction of Chinese dynasties
Level VII   Introduction of famous Chinese people, inventions, and events
Level VIII Introduction of Chinese idioms and phrases

"Chinese for Children" A coloring and activity book

"Chinese Learning Games, 10 in 1" A game set contains ten different levels learning games from recognizing characters and words to making sentences.

CD and cassettes are available for all levels.

教 材 與 教 法 簡 介

本書全套總共十冊，初級一和初級二注重趣味性，適用幼兒或初學者。第一至四冊內容以日常生活會話為主，五至八冊則著重歷史文化。全書生字共約1200個，是以倒金字塔方式逐步累積，課文的設計盡量前後聯貫，配合生字、生詞不同形式反覆練習。練習題同時函蓋讀、說、寫。每一單元可分兩個階段進行；首先做生字、生詞介紹，老師帶領學生熟悉讀音、字義之後，學生在課堂上做生字、生詞練習，以便老師觀察學生筆劃順序，並及時糾正。第二階段以說話為主，在學生交換訂正前一堂課的家庭作業之後進行；一方面復習前一堂課內容，同時為說話練習做準備。另有兒童中文一冊包含著色及記憶遊戲等，適用學齡前兒童。

訓練聽和說的上課技巧大體上有～問答、訪問、自我介紹、猜謎、說故事、遊戲、演戲或實地操作等方式。老師可依照課文內容選擇適合方式進行。（請參考「遊戲學中文」一書）

在授課過程中，對於各種形式的問題，盡量由學生回答，再由老師更正或補充，以提供學生思考機會。翻譯部分，只要意思相通，不必拘泥於特定句型結構，使學習過程更有彈性。如果有遺忘的生字、生詞也鼓勵學生使用每冊後面所附的拼音或英文索引，以便培養獨立學習的精神。

內 容 綱 要

初級一	遊戲中學聽、說、讀
初級二	遊戲中學聽、說、讀
第一冊	國籍、姓名、年級、家人、朋友…
第二冊	自我介紹（身體部位、高、矮、胖、瘦…）
第三冊	興趣、職業（動物、愛好、日期、打電話…）
第四冊	日常生活會話（購物、問路、寫信、時間…）
第五冊	文化一:中國的重要節日介紹
第六冊	文化二:中國歷代簡介
第七冊	文化三:中國重要人事物
第八冊	文化四:成語典故介紹

【兒童中文】　　　　著色、連連看、記憶遊戲等。
【實用中文遊戲】　遊戲盒，包含聽說讀十種不同程度遊戲。
【遊戲學中文】　提供家長及老師50種遊戲點子，提升學習效果。

本書特別感謝Mary Ann Davis女士的英文校對，同時以她任教資優兒童班多年經驗，對本書提供了許多寶貴意見。

第四册目次
Table of Contents

生字表
Characters you will learn from each chapter

找家教

鈴＼林金鈴　　　龍＼李小龍　　　媽＼林媽媽　　　人＼生人(Stranger)

會話（一）

（打錯電話）

龍；喂，請問是林阿姨嗎？

人＼不是，這兒不姓林。

龍＼對不起，我打錯電話了。

＊＊＊＊＊＊＊＊＊＊＊＊＊＊＊＊＊＊＊＊＊＊＊＊＊＊＊＊＊＊＊＊

（不在家）

龍＼喂，請問是林公館嗎？

媽＼是啊！你找哪位？

龍＼阿姨，我是小龍啊！表姐在嗎？

媽＼是小龍啊！你媽媽好嗎？什麼時候來美國的？為什麼沒有先通知一聲？

龍＼剛到沒幾天。媽媽說過幾天來看您。

媽＼太好了！你等一下，我去看看小鈴在不在。

龍＼好，謝謝阿姨。

媽＼喂，小龍，你表姐剛剛才出去，等一下她回來，我叫她打電話給你。你的電話幾號？

龍＼我的電話是五九四三七六八。

媽＼好，我記下來了，等她一回來，我馬上叫她打給你。

龍＼謝謝您姨媽。

媽＼不客氣，再見。

龍＼再見。

1

會話（二）

（回電話）

鈴＼喂，是小龍嗎？我是金鈴啊！

龍＼嗨！表姐你回來了。

鈴＼剛剛到家，媽說你打電話找我，什麼事？

龍＼我有事想<u>麻煩</u>你；你星期三晚上有沒<u>有空</u>？

鈴＼星期三晚上……，你先<u>告訴</u>我什麼事。

龍＼是這樣子的，我們才來美國沒<u>多久</u>，我的英文你是<u>知道</u>的，我想請你幫我<u>補</u>英文。

鈴＼好啊！<u>沒問題</u>，一個<u>鐘頭</u>多少錢？

龍＼……

鈴＼跟你<u>開玩笑</u>的，表姐怎麼會跟你要錢！

龍＼謝謝表姐！

鈴＼<u>考完試</u>再謝我吧！

Look at the pinyin and read out loud the following new words three times before doing the exercise:

New words

Aunt	wrong	resident	cousin	first	to inform	just arrived	write down
阿姨	錯	公館	表姐	先	通知	剛到	記下
ā yí	cuò	gōng guǎn	biǎo jiě	xiān	tōng zhī	gāng dào	jì xià

at once	you're welcome	to bother	available	to tell	for how long	to know
馬上	不客氣	麻煩	有空	告訴	多久	知道
mǎ shàng	bú kè qì	má fán	yǒu kòng	gào sù	duō jiǔ	zhī dào

help	to tutor	hour	money	no problem	test	to joke	you	tutor
幫	補	鐘頭	錢	沒問題	考試	開玩笑	您	家教
bāng	bǔ	zhōng tóu	qián	méi wèn tí	kǎo shì	kāi wán xiào	nín	jiā jiào

Something you need to know

A. The use of 阿姨 *aunt:*

阿姨 is used to address a lady who is about your mother's age. Or, it can be used to address your mother's sister. That is what we have used in this chapter. (姨媽 can only be used to address your mother's sister.)

B. The use of 表姐 *cousin*:

Although the meaning of 表姐 is cousin, 表姐 is used only for the female elder cousins. The elder male cousin is 表哥 the younger female cousin is called 表妹 and the younger male cousin is 表弟。However, these terms are only applied to the mother's side of the family.

C. The use of 您 *you*:

您 is a polite form of *you*. It is used to address the elder generation or to show someone your respect.
For example: 您好嗎？*How are you?*

D. The empty words 吧、啊 are meaningless and are usually used at the end of a sentence.

For example: 　給我吧！*Give it to me!* Is equivalent to 給我！

好吧！*OK!* Is equivalent to 好！

是我啊！*It's me!* Is equivalent to 是我！

你好啊！*How are you!* Is equivalent to 　　你好!

I. Fill in the blanks with appropriate English meaning.

1. 表姐 _____

2. 麻煩 _____

3. 沒問題 _____

4. 阿姨 _____

5. 通知 _____

6. 開玩笑 _____

7. 告訴 _____

8. 不客氣 _____

9. 考試 _____

10. 馬上 _____

II. Match the Chinese expressions with their English meaning.

1. 對不起，這兒不姓林 _____

A. OK, I have written it down.

2. 對不起，我打錯電話了 _____

B. You are welcome.

3. 請問是林公館嗎 _____

C. Why didn't you inform me in advance.

4. 為什麼沒有先通知一聲 _____

D. I need to ask for your help with my English.

5. 剛到沒幾天 _____

6. 你的電話幾號 _____

E. What is your telephone number?

F. Tell me what do you want first.

7. 你等一下，我去看看她在不在 _____

G. Wait a second, let me see if she is in.

8. 剛剛才出去 _____

9. 我叫她打電話給你 _____

H. Sorry, I had a wrong number.

I. How much an hour?

10. 好，我記下來了 _____

J. Sorry, this is not Lin's.

11. 等她一回來，我馬上叫她打 給你 _____

K. Is this Lin's resident?

L. Thank me after you finish the test.

12. 不客氣 _____

13. 我有事想麻煩你，你星期三 晚上有沒有空 _____

M. Once she gets home, I'll tell her to call you.

14. 你先告訴我什麼事 _____

N. I am joking. How could I ask you for the money?

15. 我想請你幫我補英文 _____

O. I need to bother you for something. Will you be available on Wednesday evening?

16. 一個鐘頭多少錢 _____

17. 跟你開玩笑的，表姐怎麼
    會跟你要錢

    P. *She just left.*

    ——— Q. *I'll tell her to call you.*

18. 考完試再謝我吧

    ——— R. *(We) just arrived a few days ago.*

III. Written exercise.
Follow the stroke order and write a complete character in each box.

阿　阿阿阿阿阿阿阿
ā

姨姨姨姨姨姨姨姨姨
yí　姨

錯錯錯錯錯錯錯錯
cuò　錯錯錯錯

公公公公公公
gōng

館館館館館館館館館
guǎn　館館館館館館

表表表表表表表表
biǎo

先先先先先先先
xiān

阿	阿		
姨	姨		
錯	錯		
公	公		
館	館		
表	表		
先	先		

知 知 知 矢 矢 知 知 知
zhī

剛 剛 岡 岡 岡 岡 岡 剛
gāng

您 您 您 佟 您 您 您 您 您
nín

馬 馬 馬 馬 馬 馬
mǎ

客 客 客 客 客 客 客 客
kè

知	知		
剛	剛		
您	您		
馬	馬		
客	客		

Write in Chinese for each given phrase.

1. Aunt: _____ _____

2. Resident: _____ _____

3. Female elder cousin: _____ _____

4. To inform: _____ _____

5. Just arrived: _____ _____

6. To write down: _____ _____

7. At once: _____ _____

8. You're welcome:_____ _____ _____

Fill in the blanks according to the given meaning.

龍：喂，請問是 _____ 嗎？

Dragon: Hello, is this aunt Lin please?

人：對不起，這兒不姓林。

People: Sorry, this is not Lin's.

龍：_____

Dragon: *Sorry, I had a wrong number.*

龍：_____

Dragon: *Hello, is this Lin's resident please?*

媽：是啊！你找哪位？

龍：阿姨＿＿＿＿在嗎？

媽：什麼時候來美國的，為什麼
沒有 ＿＿＿＿＿＿＿＿＿＿＿ ？

龍：＿＿＿＿＿ 沒幾天。

媽：你表姐 ＿＿＿＿＿＿＿ ，
等一下我叫她打電話給你。
你的 ＿＿＿＿＿＿＿＿＿＿ ？

媽：我 ＿＿＿＿＿＿＿＿等她一
回來，我 ＿＿＿＿＿叫她打
給你。

龍：＿＿＿＿＿ ，姨媽。

媽：＿＿＿＿＿ ，再見。

龍：再見。

Mom: Yes, who do you want to speak to?
Dragon: Aunt, *is (female) cousin there?*
Mom*:* When did you come to the United? *Why didn't you inform us first?*

Dragon: (We) just arrived few days ago.
Mom: *Your cousin just went out.* I'll tell her to call you later. *What is your phone number?*

Mom: *I have written it down.* As soon as she returns, *I'll tell her to call you at once.*

Dragon: *Thank you*, aunt.

Mom: *You're welcome*, goodbye.

Dragon: Goodbye.

找家教

7

麻 麻 麻 麻 麻 麻 麻 麻 麻　　麻　麻
má

煩 煩 煩 煩 煩 煩 煩 煩 煩　　煩　煩
fán

空 空 空 空 空 空 空 空 空　　空　空
kòng

告 告 告 告 告 告 告 告　　告　告
gào

訴 訴 訴 訴 訴 訴 訴 訴 訴　　訴　訴
sù

久 久 久 久　　久　久
jiǔ

幫 幫 幫 幫 幫 幫 幫 幫 幫　　幫　幫
bāng

補 補 補 補 補 補 補　　補　補
bǔ

錢 錢 錢 錢 錢 錢 錢 錢 錢　　錢　錢
qián

題 題 題 題 題 題 題 題 題　　題　題
tí

笑 笑 笑 笑 笑 笑 笑 笑 笑　　笑　笑
xiào

跟 跟 跟 跟 跟 跟 跟 跟　　跟　跟
gēn

考 考 考 考 考 考
kǎo

試 試 試 試 試 試 試
shì

道 道 道 道 道 道 道
dào

考	考		
試	試		
道	道		

Write in Chinese for each given phrase.

1. To bother: _____ _____

2. Available: _____ _____

3. To tell: _____ _____

4. How long: _____ _____

5. To know: _____ _____

6. To help me: _____ _____

7. To tutor: _____

8. Problem: _____ _____

9. Hour: _____ _____

10. How much: _____ ____ _____

11. To joke: _____ ____ _____

12. Test: _____ _____

Fill in the blanks according to the given meaning.

龍：我有事想———————— 你
，你星期三有沒有_____ ？

鈴：你 _____ 我什麼事？

龍：我的英文你是 _____
的，我想請你_____英文。

鈴：好啊！ _____ ，一個
_____ ？

_____

Dragon: *I need to bother you with something. Are you available on Wednesday evening?*
Ling: *Tell me what the matter is first?*
Dragon: *You know my English, I need to ask for your help with my English.*

Ling: OK! *No problem, how much an hour?*

鈴：_____
的，表姐怎麼會跟你要錢！

龍：謝謝表姐！

鈴：_____

Ling: *I am just joking.* How could your cousin ask you for money!

Long: Thank you cousin.

Ling: *Thank me after you finish the test.*

IV. Read the pinyin and write in Chinese.

1. Wei, Qing wen shi Lin gong guan ma? _____

2. Shi a! Ni zhao nei wei? _____

3. Ni shen me shi hou lai mei guo de, zen me bu xian tong zhi yi sheng?

   _____

4. Gang dao mei ji tian. Wo guo ji tian lai kan nin.

   _____

5. Qing deng yi xia, wo qu kan kan ta zai bu zai?

   _____

6. Biao jie gang gang cai chu qu, deng yi xia ta yi hui lai wo ma shang jiao ta da dian hua gei ni.

   _____

   _____

7. Ni de dian hua ji hao? Wo na bi ji xia lai.

   _____

8. Bu ke qi, yi ma. _____

9. Wo you shi xiang ma fan nin, ming tian nin you mei you kong?

   _____

10. Ni xian gao su wo shen me shi. _____
    Ni zhi dao wo cai lai Mei guo mei duo jiu.

    _____

11. Wo xiang qing ni bang wo bu shu xue.

_____

12. Mei wen ti, yi ge zhong tou duo shao qian?

_____

13. Gen ni kai wan xiao de. _____

V. What would you say under the following situation? (Write in Chinese)

1. You got a phone call asking for someone who doesn't live here.

_____

2. Tell someone to wait while you go to check if your mother is home or not.

_____

3. Tell the person that your father **just** went out, and **as soon as** he returns you will tell him to call him back **at once.** _____

_____

4. When people say thank you to you what do you say?

_____

5. Tell your friend that you need to **bother** her for something.

_____

6. You want to know Lin bobo's phone number.

_____

7. You need to ask someone's **help** for **tutoring** math.

_____

8. When someone agrees to help you and wants to know how much you pay him per hour. What would he say to you?

_____

9. Tell someone to thank you **later.**

_____

VI. Create a dialog according to the given sentences.

Dragon: *Hello, is this Lin's resident?* 龍： _____

People: *Sorry, you had a wrong number.* 人： _____

Dragon: *Is your phone number 345 6789?* ＿： _____

People: *Yes, but this is not Lin's.* ： _____

Dragon: *Is there a Miss. Lin?* ＿： _____

Lin: *Yes, I am. Who are you please?* 林： _____

Dragon: *Cousin, this is little Dragon.* ＿： _____

Lin: *Hey, little dragon. When did you come to the United States?* ： _____

Dragon: *I just arrived few days ago.* ＿： _____

Lin: *Why didn't you inform me in advance?* ： _____

Dragon: *I didn't want to bother you. Will you be available on Wednesday evening? I want to come to see you.* ＿： _____
_____

Lin: *OK, but I'll come to pick you up. Where do you live?* ： _____

Dragon: *Tell me first what are you doing here.* ： _____

Lin: *I am helping a girl here tutoring her English.* ＿： _____

Dragon: *Good, how much an hour?* ： _____

Lin: *????????*

Dragon: *I am joking.* ＿： _____

VII. Chapter context in pinyin and in English.

Zhao jia jia *Looking for a tutor*

(Wrong number)

Lin: lin jin ling	Long: Li xiao long	Ma: Lin ma ma	Ren: sheng ren
Lin: JinLin Lin	*Dragon: Little Dragon Li*	*Mom: Mother Lin*	*Man: Stranger*

Hui hua (yi) *Dialog (I)*

Long: Wei, qing wen shi lin a yi ma?   *Dragon: Hello, is this aunt Lin, please?*

Ren: Dui bu qi, zhe er bu xing lin.   *Man: Sorry this is not Lin's*

Long: Dui bu qi, wo da cuo dian hua le. *Dragon: Sorry, I had a wrong number.*

· ·

(Bu zai jia)	(Not home)
Long: Wei, qing wen shi Lin gong guan ma?	Dragon: *Hello, is this Lin's resident?*
Ma: Shi a! Ni zhao nei wei?	Mom: *Yes, whom do you want to speak to?*
Long: A yi, wo shi xiao long a! Biao jie zai ma?	Dragon: *Aunt, I am little dragon. Is cousin there?*
Ma: Shi xiao Long a! Ni ma ma hao ma? Shen me shi hou lai mei guo de, zen me mei you xian tong zhi yi sheng?	Mom: *Little dragon, how is your mom? when did you come to the U.S.A, and why didn't you inform me in advance?*
Long: Gang dao mei ji tian. Ma ma shuo Guo ji tian lai kan nin.	Dragon: *We just arrived few days ago. Mom said that she would come to see you later.*
Ma: Tai hao le! Ni deng yi xia, wo qu kan kan xiao Ling zai bu zai.	Mom: *It is wonderful! Wait a second, I'll go to check if little Ling is home.*
Long: Hao, xie xie a yi.	Dragon: *OK! Thank you aunt.*
Ma: Wei, xiao Long, ni biao jie gang gang cai chu qu, deng yi xia ta hui lai , wo jiao ta da dian hua gei ni, ni de dian hua ji hao?	Mom: *Hello, little dragon, your cousin just went out. Later when she returns, I'll tell her to return your call. What is your telephone number?*
Long: Wo de dian hua shi wu jiu si san qi liu ba.	Dragon: *My number is 5943768.*
Ma: Hao, wo ji xia lai le, deng ta yi hui Lai, wo ma shang jiao ta da gei ni.	Mom: *OK! I have written it down. As soon as she returns, I'll tell her to call you at once.*
Long: xie xie nin, yi ma.	Dragon: *Thank you aunt.*
Ma: Bu ke qi, zai jian.	Mom: *You're welcome, goodbye.*
Long: Zai jian.	Dragon: *Good-bye.*

13

Hui hua (er) *Dialog (ll)*

(Hui dian hua) *Returning phone call*

Ling: Wei, shi xiao long ma? Wo shi
Jin Ling a !

Ling: Hello, is this little dragon?
This is Jin Ling!

Long: Hai! Biao jie ni hui lai le.

Dragon: Hei, cousin you have returned.

Ling: Gang gang dao jia, ma shuo ni da
dian hua zhao wo, shen me shi?

Ling: I just arrived home. Mom told me that
you called me. What's the matter?

Long: Wo you shi xiang ma fan ni, ni
Xing qi san wan shang you mei you
kong?

Dragon: I need to bother you for something. Will
you be available on Wednesday evening?

Ling: Xing qi san wan shang....., ni
xian gao su wo shen me shi.

Ling: Wednesday evening........, tell me what is
the matter first.

Long: Shi zhe yang zi de, wo men cai lai
Mei guo mei duo jiu, wo de ying wen ni
Shi zhi dao de, wo xiang qing ni bang wo
Bu ying wen.

Dragon: It is that we just arrived in the U.S.A
and you know my English, I need to ask
for your help to tutor me English.

Ling: Hao a! Mei wen ti, yi ge zhong tou
Duo shao qian?

Ling: OK! No problem, how much per hour?

Long: ....

Dragon: ....

Ling: Gen ni kai wan xiao de, biao jie zen
Me hui gen ni yao qian!

Ling: I am joking, how can a cousin ask you
for money!

Long: Xie xie biao jie!

Dragon: Thank you cousin!

Ling: Kao wan shi zai xie wo ba!

Lin: Thank me after you finish the test.

VIII. Oral exercise
Use the given scenarios to create your own telephone conversation with a friend or an adult.

a. You got a phone call that was a wrong number.
b. You called a friend, but her mother answered the phone and said that she
   was not home.
c. You are telling your aunt that your mother is not home, but you will tell
    her to return your aunt's phone call at once as soon as she gets home.
d. You ask aunt's phone number and write it down.

打電話

李＼先生，請問哪兒有公用電話？

王＼我記得這附近有一個公用電話。你在這兒等一下，
　　我去看看，馬上回來。

王＼公共汽車站外面有一個公用電話，我帶你去。

李＼謝謝你，先生。請問您貴姓？

王＼我姓王，國王的王，你呢？

李＼我姓李，木、子李，剛從美國回來。我想打電話給
　　表哥，請他來接我。

王＼你的表哥住在附近嗎？還是你要打長途電話？

李＼我表哥說他家到車站，開車只要五分鐘。

王＼所以，你不是要打長途電話。因為用公用電話打長
　　途電話太貴了。

李＼打本地電話要多少錢？

王＼先放五塊錢，等電話接通以後，也許還要加錢，也許不用。

李＼五塊錢！這麼貴！

王＼小姐，不是美金五塊錢，放心，是台幣五塊錢。

公用電話

公共汽車＝公車＝Bus

15

New words

Mister	先生	xiān shēng
long distance	長途	cháng tú
public phone	公用電話	gōng yòng diàn huà
remember	記得	jì dé
outside	外面	wài miàn
male cousin	表哥	biǎo gē
local	本地	běn dì

expensive	貴	guì
honorable surname	貴姓	guì xìng
king	國王	guó wáng
station	車站	chē zhàn
don't worry	放心	fàng xīn
Li	李	lǐ
Taiwan dollar	台幣	tái bì

from	從	cóng
perhaps	也許	yě xǔ
add	加	jiā
American dollar	美金	měi jīn
miss	小姐	xiǎo jiě
a piece	塊	kuài
five dollars	五塊錢	wǔ kuài qián

I. Match the Chinese phrases with their English meaning.

1. 先生　　【　】
2. 公用電話【　】
3. 記得　　【　】
4. 公共汽車【　】
5. 車站　　【　】
6. 外面　　【　】
7. 國王　　【　】
8. 貴姓　　【　】
9. 表哥　　【　】

10. 長途電話【　】
11. 太貴了　【　】
12. 本地　　【　】
13. 也許　　【　】
14. 五塊錢　【　】
15. 美金　　【　】
16. 放心　　【　】
17. 台幣　　【　】
18. 小姐　　【　】

A. American dollars
B. Bus
C. Outside
D. cousin
E. Five dollars
F. Don't worry
G. Too expensive

H. Local
I. Perhaps
J. Mister
K. Miss
L. King
M. Honorable surname

N. Long distance
O. Taiwan dollars
P. Remember
Q. Public phone
R. Bus station

II. Follow the stroke order and write the complete character in each box.

共共共共共共
gòng

站站立站站站
zhàn

面面面面面面面
miàn

貴貴貴貴貴貴貴
guì

李李李李李李李李
lǐ

從從從從從從從從
cóng

汽汽汽汽汽
qì

途途途途途途途
tú

許許許許許許
xǔ

加加加加加加
jiā

台台台台
tái

幣幣幣幣幣幣幣幣
bì

塊塊塊塊塊塊塊塊
kuài

III. Write in Chinese for the following phrases.

1. Mister: _____ _____

2. Miss: _____ _____

3. Bus: ___ ___ ___ ___

4. Bus station: ___ ___

5. Public phone: ___ ___ ___ ___

6. Cousin: _____ _____

7. Outside: _____ _____

8. Perhaps: ___ ___

9. Too expensive: ___ ___ ___

10. Five dollars: ___ ___ ___

11. American dollar: ___ ___

12. Taiwan dollar: ___ ___

13. Don't worry: ___ ___

14. Local: ___ ___

15. Long distance: ___ ___

16. King: ___ ___

17. Honorable surname: ___ ___

18. Remember: ___ ___

IV. Fill in the blanks by using the words in section III.

1. _____，請問哪兒有公用電話？

2. 我 _____ 這附近有一個公用電話。

3. _____站外面有一個公用電話。

4. 請問您 ────────── ？

5. 我姓王，_____ 的王。

6. 我想請 _____ 來接我。

7. 表哥說他家到 _____ 開車只要五分鐘。

8. 用公用電話打長途電話 _____ 了。

9. 打 _____ 電話多少錢？

10. 電話接通後 _____ 還要加錢，也許不用。

11. 不是美金 _____ ，放心是_____ 五塊錢。

12. 用公用電話打_____ 太貴了。

V. Answer the questions according to the real situation.

1. 阿姨的孩子男生叫 _____ 或是 _____
   女生叫 _____ 或是 _____

2. 你有幾個表哥？ _____ 幾個表姐？_____

3. 你家附近有沒有公共汽車站？_____

4. 你會不會打公用電話？ _____

5. 美國打一通公用電話最少要放多少錢？_____

6. 你有沒有打過家裏的電話？ _____

7. 外婆的電話是長途電話還是本地電話？ _____

8. 家裏長途電話打得多還是本地電話？ _____

9. 現在打長途電話是不是比以前貴？ _____

VI.   Translate the following into Chinese.

1. Mister, may I ask where a public phone is?

2. I remember there is a bus station in this neighborhood.

3. She uses the public phone to make a long distance phone call.

4. Miss, may I ask what your honorable surname is?

5. The king of England can't make long distance calls.

6. This movie ticket is too expensive.

7. How much is the bus ticket?

8. Don't worry, it is Taiwan dollar not American dollar.

VI.   Oral exercise.

Tell or ask an adult

a. How much it is to make a local phone call from a public phone.
b. Whether it is a long distance or a local call to call your grandma.
c. If it is very expensive to make a long distance call.
d. What is her (or his) honorable surname.

Chapter context in pinyin

Da dian hua

Li: Xian sheng, qing wen na er you gong yong dianhua?

Wang: Wo ji de zhe fu jin you yi ge gong yong dian hua. Ni zai zher deng
yi xia, wo qu kan kan, ma shang hui lai.

Li: Xie xie ni, xian sheng. Qing wen nin gui xing?

Wang: Wo xing wang, guo wang de wang, Ni ne?

Li: Wo xing Li, mu, zi Li, gang cong Mei Guo hui lai. Wo xiang da dian
hua gei biao ge, qing ta lai jie wo.

Wang: Ni de biao ge zhu zai fu jin ma? Hai shi ni yao da chang tu dian hua?

Li: Wo biao ge shuo ta jia dao che zhan, kai che zhi yao wu fen zhong.

Wang: Suo yi, ni bu shi yao da chang tu dian hua. Yin wei yong gong yong
dian hua da chang tu dian hua tai gui le.

Li: Da ben di dian hua yao duo shao qian?

Wang: xian fang wu kuai qian, deng dian hua jie tong yi hou, ye xu hai yao
jia qian, ye xu bu yong.

Li: Wu kuai qian! Zhen me gui!

Wang: xiao jie, bu shi Mei jin wu kuai qian, fang xin, shi tai bi wu kuai qian.

Translation of the chapter contents

Making a phone call

Li: Mister, may I ask where is the public phone?

*Wang: I remember there is one in the neighborhood. Wait a moment here, I
go to check, and will be back at once.*

Wang: There is one outside the bus station. I'll take you there.

Li: Thank you mister. May I ask your honorable surname?

Wang: My last name is Wang, The Wang of king, And you?

*Li: My surname is Li, wood and son Li, just came back from the United
States. I want to call my cousin to come to pick me up.*

*Wang: Does your cousin live around here? Or do you want to make a long
distance call?*

*Li: My cousin said that it only takes five minutes to drive from his house to
the bus station.*

*Wang: So you are not making a long distance call. Because to use the
public phone to make the long distance call is too expensive.*

Li: How much is the local call?

*Wang: Put five dollars first. After the line is connected, perhaps you need to
add in more, perhaps you don't.*

Li: Five dollars! So expensive!

*Wang: Miss, it is not five American dollars. Don't worry, it is five Taiwan
dollars.*

21

買車票

李　　　：先生我想買一張去台南的火車票。

售票員：小姐你要買普通車票還是直達車票？

李　　　：有什麼不一樣？

售票員：普通車每站都停，直達車中間不停，直達台南。直達車比普通車快得多。

李　　　：直達車票一張多少錢？

售票員：四百五十塊錢一張單程票。

李　　　：普通車呢？多少錢一張？

售票員：普通車單程票兩百二十塊錢一張，來回票也就是雙程票四百四十塊錢一張。

李　　　：好，我買一張普通車來回票。

李　　　：請問火車什麼時候開？什麼時候到台南？

售票員：火車時間表在售票亭外面，你可以自己去看。

李　　　：謝謝你。

售票員：不客氣。

不一樣：diffferent　　　來回back & forth =雙程round trip

New words

Tainan	train ticket	ticket-seller	ticket booth	buy	regular train
台南	火車票	售票員	售票亭	買	普通車
tái nán	huǒ chē piào	shòu piào yuán	shòu piào tíng	mǎi	pǔ tōng chē

Express train	stop	middle	one way	round trip	hundred	schedule
直達車	停	中間	單程	雙程	百	時間表
zhí dá chē	tíng	zhōng jiān	dān chéng	shuāng chéng	bǎi	shí jiān biǎo

I.   Match the Chinese phrases with their English meaning.

1. 台南 _____
2. 火車票 _____
3. 售票員 _____
4. 售票亭 _____
5. 普通車 _____
6. 直達車 _____
7. 中間 _____

8. 單程 _____
9. 雙程 _____
10. 買票 _____
11. 時間表 _____
12. 兩百 _____
13. 停 _____

A. *Express train*
B. *Middle*
C. *Buy tickets*
D. *Round trip*

E. *One way*
F. *Tainan*
G. *Train ticket*
H. *Regular train*

I. *Ticket booth*
J. *Ticket seller*
K. *Stop*
L. *Two hundred*
M. *Schedule*

Something you need to know

台南*Tainan* is one of the major cities in Taiwan. It is located in the south part of Taiwan. 南*nan* means south, 台 *tai* means Taiwan,台南 is in south Taiwan. There are other cities in Taiwan such as 台北，台中 these names also refer to the locations.

23

II. Follow the stroke order and write a complete character in each box.

買買買買買買
mǎi

南南南南南南南
nán

火火火火
huǒ

員員員員員員
yuán

售售售售售售售
shòu

亭亭亭亭亭亭亭
tíng

普普普普普普普
pǔ

直直直直直直直
zhí

達達達達達達達
dá

停停停
tíng

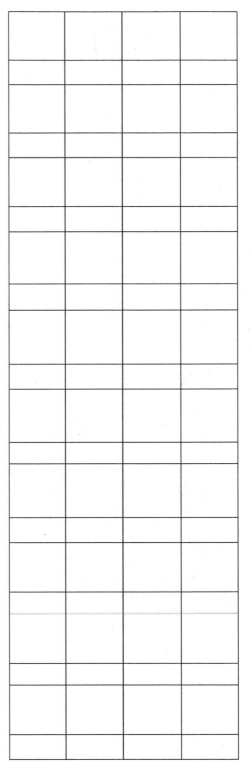

間 間 間 間 間 間 間
jiān

單 單 單 單 單 單
dān

程 程 程 程 程 程 程
chéng

百 百 百 百 百
bǎi

III.   Write in Chinese for the given phrases.

1. Buy: _____

2. Train ticket: _____ _____ _____

3. Ticket-seller: _____ _____ _____

4. Regular train (car): _____ _____ _____

5. Express train (car): _____ _____ _____

6. One way: _____ _____

7. Round trip: _____ _____

8. Schedule: _____ _____ _____

9. Ticket booth: _____ _____ _____

10. Middle: _____ _____

11. Two hundred dollars: _____ _____ _____ _____

12. Tainan: _____ _____

IV.   Fill in the blanks according to the word given.

1. 我想買一張從_____ 到 _____ 的車票。(Taipei, Tainan)

2. 請問_____ 在哪兒？(Ticket booth)

3. 問那位_____ 就知道了(Ticket-seller)

4.. —————— 比 —————— 快得多。(Express train, regular train)

5.. —————— 一張多少錢？(One way ticket)

6.. —————— 一張兩百三十塊錢。(Round trip)

7.. —————— 比較貴(Express train ticket)

8. 直達車 ———— 不停(middle)

9. 火車 ———— 就在車站 ———— . (schedule, outside)

10. 直達車中間不 ——。(stop)

V. What would you say in the following situation?
(Fill in the boxes with the sentences you create.)

1. You want to buy a round trip train ticket.

2. Ask people where the ticket-booth is. *(Use polite form; qing wen)*

3. Ask people who the ticket-seller is. *(Use polite form; qing wen and na wei)*

		.					

4. You want to know where the train schedule is.

5. You want to know what is the difference between express and regular trains.

		和					不	一	
		和					不	一	

6. The express train is faster.

26

7. The regular train will stop in the middle.

					會	

8. (This) train ticket (is) two hundred thirty five *dollars* Taiwan dollars.

VI.　Unscramble the sentences.

1. 到台南　　　從台北　　　要多久

＿＿＿＿＿＿＿＿＿＿＿＿＿＿＿＿＿＿＿＿＿

2. 什麼時候　　普通車　　到台中

＿＿＿＿＿＿＿＿＿＿＿＿＿＿＿＿＿＿＿＿＿

3. 直達車　　可是　　比較貴　　比較快

＿＿＿＿＿＿＿＿＿＿＿＿＿＿＿＿＿＿＿＿＿

4. 售票員　　外面　　就站(stand)在　　售票亭

＿＿＿＿＿＿＿＿＿＿＿＿＿＿＿＿＿＿＿＿＿

5. 兩百七十九　　一張　　塊錢　　單程火車票

＿＿＿＿＿＿＿＿＿＿＿＿＿＿＿＿＿＿＿＿＿

6. 自己去　　你可以　　時間表　　在外面　　看

＿＿＿＿＿＿＿＿＿＿＿＿＿＿＿＿＿＿＿＿＿

VII.　Oral exercise (Practice with a friend or an adult)

Make up a dialog with a friend. Pretend you are going to Tainan and you are buying a round trip ticket from your friend who pretends to be the ticket seller. Find out how much a one-way and a round trip ticket costs and what the difference is.

寫給外婆的信

親愛的外婆：

您好嗎？我很好！

您寄來的禮物，我收到了，謝謝您！

昨天，爸爸帶我們去南部玩。一大早，我們就到火車站，買了四張直達車單程票。不久火車就來了。

本來要買雙程票，但是因為假日關係，所有的票都賣光了，我們只好到達台南後，再買回程票。
直達車很快就到台南了。一下車，爸爸馬上就去售票亭買票。結果只買到普通車票，而且，回程票比較貴，比來的時候貴了五十塊錢。可是售票員說假日期間能買到票已經很不錯了。
外婆，我真希望您也和我們一起去台南。我和弟弟都好想念您，您什麼時候再來看我們呢？

敬祝

外婆健康快樂

孫
國聲
敬上

New words

Letter	to mail	holiday	originally	all of	sold out	arrived	dear
信	寄	假日	本來	所有的	賣光	到達	親愛的
xìn	jì	jià rì	běn lái	suǒ yǒu de	mài guāng	dào dá	qīn ài de

Not bad	to miss	relation	as a result	a period of time	happy	healthy	not long
不錯	想念	關係	結果	期間	快樂	健康	不久
bú cuò	xiǎng niàn	guān xi	jié guǒ	qí jiān	kuài lè	jiàn kāng	bù jiǔ

To wish respectfully	to present respectfully	grandchild	return trip ticket
敬祝	敬上	孫／孫子	回程票
jìng zhù	jìng shàng	sūn/sūn zi	huí chéng piào

I. Match the Chinese expressions with their English meaning.

1. 敬祝＼ _____

2. 寄信＼ _____

3. 假日＼ _____

4. 回程票 _____

5. 健康＼ _____

6. 親愛的＼_____

7. 不錯＼ _____

8. 孫＼ _____

9. 敬上＼ _____

10. 想念＼ _____

11. 關係＼ _____

12. 結果＼ _____

13. 期間＼ _____

14. 到達＼ _____

15. 賣光＼ _____

16. 所有的＼ _____

17. 本來＼ _____

18. 快樂＼ _____

A. To present
   respectfully
B. To mail letter
C. Happy
D. Healthy
E. Dear
F. Sold out

G. Grandchild
H. Originally
I. All of
J. As a result
K. A period
L. Holiday
M. Not bad

N. To arrive
O. To miss
P. To wish
   respectfully
Q. Return trip ticket
R. Relation

29

II. Follow the stroke order and write a complete character in each box.

信信信信
xìn

親親親親親親
qīn

寄寄寄寄寄寄
jì

假假假假假假假
jià

係係係係係係
xi

賣賣賣賣賣
mài

結結結結結結結
jié

果果果果果果
guǒ

敬敬敬敬敬敬敬
jing

祝祝祝祝祝
zhù

健健健健健健
jiàn

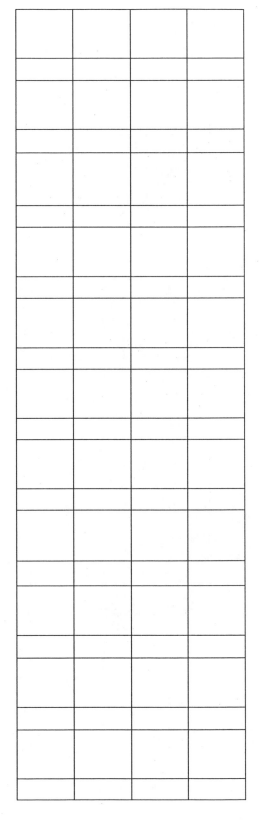

康康康康康康康康
kāng

孫孫孫孫孫孫孫
sūn

III. Write in Chinese for each given phrase.

1. Healthy: _____ _____

2. To mail a letter: _____ _____

3. All of: _____ _____ _____

4. A period: _____ _____

5. Not bad: _____ _____

6. To present respectfully: _____ _____

7. To miss: _____ _____

8. Dear: _____ _____

9. Sold out: _____ _____

10. To arrive: _____ _____

11. Holiday: _____ _____

12. Relation: _____ _____

13. Return trip ticket: ____ ____ ___

14. As a result: ____ _____

15. Grand child: ____

16. Happy: _____ _____

17. Originally: _____ _____

18. To wish respectfully: _____ _____

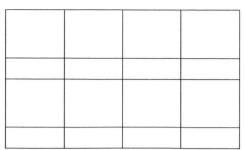

IV. Fill in the blanks using the words in section III.

1. _____外婆：近來好嗎？

2. 好久不見，我們都很 _____您。

3. 姐姐剛才出去 _____ (to mail a letter)。

4. 因為今天是 _____，學校不上課。

5. 我 _____ 要去台南玩，後來沒有去。

6. 假日 _____ 最好不要出門。

7. 你的字寫得很 _____(Not bad)。

8.＿＿＿＿＿健康快樂　　　孫 國聲＿＿＿＿＿。

9. 我是奶奶的＿＿＿＿子。

10. 媽媽希望我們每天都很 ＿＿＿＿ (healthy) 快樂。

11. 今天是媽媽的生日，祝媽媽生日 ＿＿＿＿＿ (happy).

12. 我們本來要去台中，＿＿＿＿＿ 沒有去。

13. 假日期間所有的回程車票都 ＿＿＿＿＿ 了。

14. 因為假日＿＿＿＿＿ 所有的票都賣光了。

V. Translate the following into Chinese.

1. Dear cousin: We all miss you very much. *(use female and polite form)*

2. Grandpa, the gift you sent we have **all** received.

									都			了	

3. Early in the morning we arrived (at) the train station.

4. He wants to buy the express train ticket for (to *give*) you.

5. Because of the holiday (*relation*), all of the tickets are sold out.

6. We bought the return trip ticket at the ticket booth.

		在					了			

7. As a result, we only bought two regular train tickets.

					到							

8. (We) wish you respectfully, healthy (and) happy.

VI. According to the situation, fill in the blanks with appropriate words.

寫給表姐的信

＿＿＿＿＿＿的表姐＼您好嗎？

今天是美國的假日，所有的學校都不上課，爸爸也不用上班(to work)。所以，一大早我們就去紐約(New York)。

大部份的美國人出門都開車。在中國大部份的人搭(take)公共汽車或是火車。火車有＿＿＿＿＿＿＿或是＿＿＿＿＿＿。我記得小時候的火車站賣直達車票和＿＿＿＿＿＿＿。每到＿＿＿＿＿＿時候，票最不好買，一下就＿＿＿＿＿＿了。　　　　　　　　　　　　　　　　　　　　　　＿＿＿＿＿＿

那時候車票不貴，一張＿＿＿＿＿＿＿才一百四十塊錢＿＿＿＿＿＿＿，不是美金。雙程票是＿＿＿＿＿＿＿＿＿＿台幣。

表姐我們都很＿＿＿＿＿＿，希望您能和我們一起去紐約(New York)。您什麼時候再來看我們呢？

敬祝

＿＿＿＿＿＿＿＿＿＿＿＿＿＿＿＿　　　　　　　　　　表＿＿＿

　　　　　　　　　　　　　　　　　　　　　　　　　　＿＿＿＿＿＿

　　　　　　　　　　　　　　　　　　　　　　　　　　　　＿＿＿＿＿＿

VII. Write a letter to your cousin and tell him/her about your holiday.

I.　　Oral drill
Use the listed words to replace the underlined words and read out loud.

回程票比較貴，比來的時候貴了五十塊錢。

1. 公共汽車票，火車票　　　　　4. 學跳舞，學唱歌
2. 電動玩具，小手槍　　　　　　5. 學電腦，學游泳
3. 來回票，單程票　　　　　　　6. 兒童樂園，動物園

我的<u>日記</u>

一九九九年九月二十八日　　　　　　星期二　<u>天氣</u> 晴

今天是一個<u>特別</u>的日子，因為今天是媽媽的生日，也是<u>教師節</u>。媽媽說，每年的這一天，<u>台灣</u>所有的學校都<u>放假</u>。媽媽是老師，所以也放假，她的朋友就會請她去看電影，為她<u>慶祝</u>生日。

媽媽說，教師節是為<u>紀念</u>中國最<u>偉大</u>的老師---<u>孔子</u>。
每年的這一天，台灣<u>通常</u>有慶祝<u>活動</u>，紀念這一位偉大的<u>人物</u>。

我們問媽媽，希望我們送什麼禮物給她。媽媽說：「只要你們天天都很健康快樂，做一個聽話的孩子，就是給我最好的禮物。」

晚上，爸爸帶大家去中國<u>飯館</u> 吃飯。飯後媽媽拿到的<u>幸運簽</u>寫的是 "祝你生日快樂"。

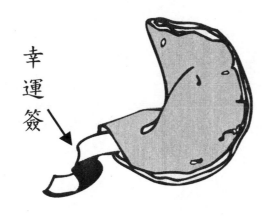

幸運簽

New words

Not raining	diary	to remember	special	teacher's day	celebrate	great
晴	日記	紀念	特別	教師節	慶祝	偉大
qíng	rì jì	jì niàn	tè bié	jiào shī jié	qìng zhù	wěi dà

Day off	Confucius	usually	activity	character	restaurant	to eat
放假	孔子	通常	活動	人物	飯館	吃
fàng jià	kǒng zǐ	tōng cháng	huó dòng	rén wù	fàn guǎn	chī

Cooked rice	lucky	a label	fortune cookie label	eat a meal	Taiwan
飯	幸運	簽	幸運簽	吃飯	台灣
fàn	xìng yùn	qiān	xìng yùn qiān	chī fàn	tái wān

I. Match each Chinese expression with an appropriate English meaning.

1. 特別： _____

2. 飯館： _____

3. 孔子： _____

4. 日記： _____

5. 紀念： _____

6. 幸運簽： _____

7. 晴： _____

8. 慶祝： _____

9. 偉人： _____

10. 教師節： _____

11. 吃飯： _____

12. 通常： _____

13. 放假： _____

14. 活動： _____

15. 人物： _____

A. Eat a meal
B. Restaurant
C. Special
D. Usually
E. Celebrate

F. Diary
G. Teacher's day
H. Character
I. To remember
J. Confucius

K. Day off
L. Not raining
M. Fortune cookie label
N. Great
O. Activity

II. Follow the stroke order and write a complete character in each box.

晴晴晴晴晴晴
qíng

節節節節節節節節
jié

特特特特特特特
tè

別別別別
bié

慶慶慶慶慶慶慶慶
qìng

紀紀紀紀紀
jì

偉偉偉偉偉偉偉
wěi

活活活活活
huó

飯飯飯飯飯飯飯
fàn

吃吃吃吃
chī

孔孔孔
kǒng

36

幸幸幸幸幸
xing

簽簽簽簽簽簽簽簽
qiān

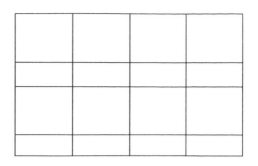

III. Write in Chinese for each given phrase.

1. Eat a meal ——— ———

2. Restaurant ——— ———

3. Special ——— ———

4. Usually ——— ———

5. Celebrate ——— ———

6. Diary ——— ———

7. Teacher's day ——— ——— ———

8. Character ——— ———

9. To remember ——— ———

10. Confucius ——— ———

11. Day off ——— ———

12. Not raining ———

13. Fortune cookie label——— ——— ———

14. Great ——— ———

15. Activity ——— ———

I. Fill in the blanks with appropriate words in the word bank.

特別，人物，晴，慶祝，教師節，偉大，吃飯，通常
飯館，紀念，孔子，幸運籤，日記，活動，放假

1. 老師叫同學們要天天寫 _____ 。

2. 今天天氣很好，沒有下雨 (raining)，是一個大 ____天。

3. 媽媽的生日，爸爸帶我們去 _____ 吃飯。

4. 每一次_____ 的時候，弟弟老是說話說不停(stop)。

5. 這一個電話亭看起來很不一樣，很 _____ 。

37

6. 九月二十八號是台灣的 —————— ，學校不上課。

7. 一月一號過新年，爸爸和媽媽都 _____ ，不用<u>上班</u>(to work)。

8. 學校有很多不同的 _____ ，例如，游泳，爬山等等。

9. 我將來長大要做一個 _____ 的 人 物 。

10.卡通片裏的許多卡通 _____ 都好可愛。

11. _____是中國最偉大的老師。

12.在中國飯館吃飯都會收到一張 _____ 。

13.教師節是 _____ 孔子的日子。

14. _____ 我們是先吃飯再打球。

15.我們通常會帶小朋友去動物園或是兒童樂園 _____兒童節。

II.　　Translate the following sentences into Chinese.

1. Today is a special day, so school is closed.(day off)

2. (On) Teacher's Day, father took us to eat in the restaurant.

3. Grandfather is a great character.

4. I usually write (in my) diary everyday.

5. On Confucius birthday, there are many celebrating activities in Taiwan.

		的			灣								

6. The lucky label tells me that my test is OK (no problem).

III. Answer the questions according to your real situation.

1. 你有沒有天天寫日記？ _____

2. 你在什麼地方看過幸運簽？ _____

3. 你的生日，爸媽帶你去哪兒慶祝？ _____

4. 教師節是什麼時候？ _____

5. 教師節是紀念誰？ _____

6. 孔子是誰？ _____

7. 在學校裏，你有沒有參加什麼活動？ _____

8. 通常你喜歡什麼天氣出門？ _____

IV. Use another piece of paper to write a diary for what happened today.

V. Oral drill
Use the listed words to replace the under lined words and read out loud.

我一<u>回家</u>就想<u>吃東西</u>

1. 上飯館，吃魚
2. 做完功課，玩電腦
3. 考試，開玩笑
4. 放假，去看電影
5. 放學，去打球
6. 到公共汽車站，打電話
7. 到售票亭，買雙程票
8. 麻煩她，給她台幣

時間

先生： 小姐，請問現在幾點鐘？

小姐： 五點半，正是下班時間路上最忙的時候。

先生： 難怪六號公車到現在還沒有來。

小姐： 六號班車最近停開了，您不知道嗎？

先生： 不知道，因為我上個月才剛從美國到台灣。

小姐： 怪不得，車站外面有最新的<u>公車</u>時刻表，我帶你去看看
。

先生： 我要去台中看親戚，打算明天下午回來。你看要搭什麼
車好？

小姐： 五點四十有一班，六點鐘也有一班，六點零五分還有一
班往台中。

先生： 如果我搭六點整這班直達車，從這兒到台中要多久？

小姐： 也許兩個鐘頭。如果六點整準時出發，八點會到。明天
回來的時候，您可以搭中午十二點整往台北的班車，剛
好下午兩點鐘到。

先生： 太好了！謝謝您！

小姐： 不客氣。

§公車＝公共汽車

New words

Half	busy	exactly so	no wonder	no wonder	schedule	departure	sharp
半	忙	正是	難怪	怪不得	時刻表	出發	整
bàn	máng	zhèng shì	nán guài	guài bù dé	shí kè biǎo	chū fā	zhěng

Relative	to plan	afternoon	if	to ride	on time	exactly	to depart
親戚	打算	下午	如果	搭	準時	剛好	往
qīn qì	dǎ suàn	xià wǔ	rú guǒ	dā	zhǔn shí	gāng hǎo	wǎng

Something you need to know

The use of time words:

早上 *(zao shang)* or 上午 Is the word for morning. For example:

       10:50 AM　早上十點五十分

       8:45 AM　上午八點四十五分

中午 *(zhong wu)* means noon that is between twelve and one o'clock.

    For example:　　12:00 PM 中午十二點整

               12:30 PM 中午十二點半（三十分）

下午 *(xia wu)* means afternoon that is around one to six o'clock.

    For example:　　2:05 PM 下午兩點零五分

               5:55 PM 下午五點五十五分

晚上 *(wan shang)* means evening or night that is the time after six PM.

    For example:　　6:30 PM晚上六點半（三十分）

             10:20 PM 晚上十點二十分

I.　Write in Chinese for the following time expressions.

1. 5:30 AM _____

2. 6:45 PM _____

3. 12:00 PM _____

4. 3:05 AM _____

5. 12:55 AM _____

6. 2:50 PM _____

II. Follow the stroke order and write a complete character in each box.

半 半 半 半
bàn

正 正 正 正 正
zhèng

忙 忙 忙 忙 忙 忙
máng

難 難 難 難 難 難 難 難
nán

怪 怪 怪 怪 怪 怪 怪
guài

刻 刻 刻 刻 刻 刻
kè

戚 戚 戚 戚 戚 戚 戚 戚
qì

算 算 算 算 算 算 算
suàn

午 午 午 午
wǔ

搭 搭 搭 搭 搭 搭
dā

準 準 準 準 準 準 準
zhǔn

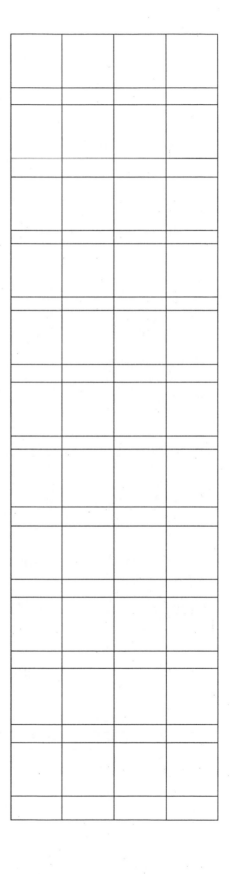

往往往往往
wǎng

整整整整整整
zhěng

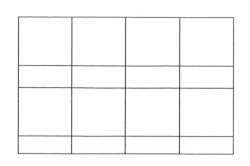

III. Write in Chinese for the following words.

1. One half: _____ _____   9. Afternoon: _____ _____

2. Exactly so: _____ _____   10.If: _____ _____

3. No wonder: _____ _____   11.To ride: _____

4. No wonder: ____ _____ _____   12.On time: _____ _____

5. Schedule: _____ _____ _____   13.Exactly: _____ _____

6. Departure: ____ _____   14.To depart: _____

7. Relative: _____ _____   15.Bus: _____ _____

8. To plan: _____ _____   16.Busy _____

IV. Translate the following sentences into Chinese.

1. May I ask, what time is it now?

2. It is exactly the time (people) getting off work, the busiest traffic hours.

3. What time do you plan to depart?

4. If the bus departs on time, we will arrive in the noon.

5. It is exactly twelve o'clock sharp.

6. No wonder my relative is **so** busy.(zhe me = so)

					這	麼	
					這	麼	

7. The new schedule is outside the bus station.

	的								
	的								

8. No wonder you want to ride the regular train/car.

								車
								車

V.   Answer the questions according to your real situation.

1. 你每天是不是搭校車上學？ _____

2. 你幾點鐘出發去校車車站？_____

3. 你有沒有每次都準時到車站？ _____

4. 你下學期還打算搭校車上學嗎？ _____

5. 你有沒有親戚住在附近？ _____

6. 去親戚家，你們自己開車還是搭公車？ _____

7. 每天下午四點整，你通常在做什麼？ _____

VI. Give responses to the following statements and questions according to the given sentences.

請問現在幾點鐘？

_____

It is Chinese time 6:30 PM now.

六路車停開了   _____

No wonder there is no number six bus on the schedule.

我要去台灣看親戚，打算明天下午回來，你看搭什麼車好？

_____

There is one at ten thirty, and one at eleven sharp, and still one at twelve noon.

如果我搭這班車，到台南要多久？

_____

Maybe two hours, maybe two and half hours.

VII. Oral drill
Use the listed words to replace the underlined words and read out loud.

    A. 我上個月才剛從<u>美國</u>到<u>台灣</u>

    B. 從<u>美國</u>到<u>台灣</u>要多久

台南，台北
美國，中國
日本，台灣
英國，美國

    C. 有<u>美金</u>，也有<u>台幣</u>，還有<u>日幣</u>

公車，火車，直達車
長途電話，本地電話，國外電話
表哥，表姐，表弟
爺爺，奶奶，外婆

問路 (一)

你： 請問<u>廁所</u>在哪兒？

他： 你走出車站往<u>右拐</u>，就會看到廁所外面掛的<u>牌子</u>，你一看 就知道了。

你： 廁所<u>旁邊</u>是不是有一個公用電話亭？

他： 對了！廁所就在公用電話亭<u>左邊</u>。

你： 我想起來了，廁所<u>前面</u>是<u>加油站</u>，對不對？

他： 對！<u>後面</u>是<u>停車場</u>。<u>別忘了</u>先去向加油站的人拿<u>鎖匙</u>。

你： 我<u>差點</u>忘了，謝謝你。

他： 不客氣。

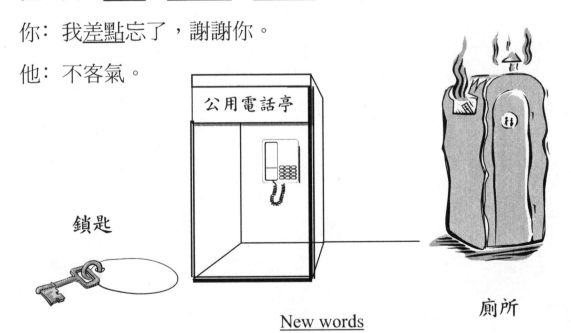

鎖匙

公用電話亭

廁所

New words

A toilet	turn	right	left	sign	the side	parking lot	key	forget
廁所	拐	右	左	牌子	旁邊	停車場	鎖匙	忘
cè suǒ	guǎi	yòu	zuǒ	pái zi	páng biān	tíng chē chǎng	suǒ shi	wàng

toward	almost	gas station	turn right	don't forget	the front	the back
向	差點	加油站	右拐	別忘了	前面	後面
xiàng	chā diǎn	jiā yóu zhàn	yòu guǎi	bié wàng le	qián miàn	hòu miàn

Exercise

I. **Follow the stroke order and write a complete character in each box.**

廁 廁 廁 廁 廁 廁
cè

右 右 右
yòu

拐 拐 拐 拐 拐
guǎi

左 左 左
zuǒ

牌 牌 牌 牌 牌 牌
pái

旁 旁 旁 旁 旁 旁
páng

邊 邊 邊 邊 邊 邊 邊
biān

油 油 油 油 油 油
yóu

場 場 場 場 場 場
chǎng

鎖 鎖 鎖 鎖 鎖 鎖 鎖 鎖
suǒ

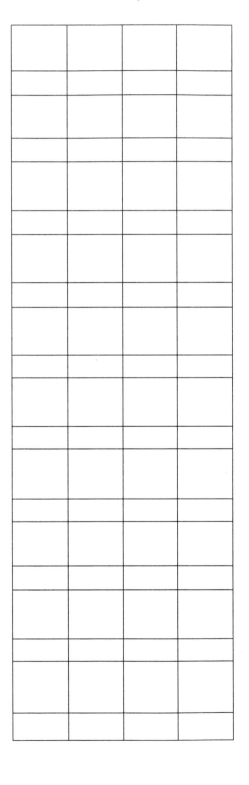

匙 匙 匙 匙 匙 匙 匙
shi

差 差 差 差 差
chā

忘 忘 忘 忘 忘
wàng

向 向 向 向
xiàng

II. Write in Chinese for the following words.

1. A toilet: ＿＿＿＿ ＿＿＿＿

2. The side: ＿＿＿＿ ＿＿＿＿

3. Turn right: ＿＿＿＿ ＿＿＿＿

4. Turn left: ＿＿＿＿ ＿＿＿＿

5. A sign: ＿＿＿＿ ＿＿＿＿

6. Gas station: ＿＿ ＿＿ ＿＿

7. Parking lot: ＿＿ ＿＿ ＿＿

8. Key: ＿＿ ＿＿

9. Almost: ＿＿＿ ＿＿＿

10. Don't forget: ＿＿ ＿＿ ＿＿

11. The back: ＿＿＿ ＿＿＿

12. The front: ＿＿＿ ＿＿＿

III. Fill in the blanks according to the chapter context.

你走出車站就會看到 ＿＿＿＿ 外面掛的＿＿＿＿，你一看就知道了。

廁所 ＿＿＿＿ 是不是公用電話亭？

對了，廁所就在公用電話亭 ＿＿＿＿。

我想起來了，廁所 ＿＿＿＿ 是 ＿＿＿＿＿，對不對？

對了！_____ 是 _____，別忘了先去向停車場的人拿 _____。

我_____忘了，謝謝你。

IV. Translate the following sentences into Chinese.

1. Walk outside toward the bus station (and then) turn right.

	出					面			

2. The public telephone booth is right on the left of it.

3. The gas station is in the front (and) the parking lot is in the back.

4. The key to the toilet **is right on your** right.

5. I almost forgot **on the side** there is a sign.

V. Write in Chinese for the places you found in the blanks.
(Look at the map and locate the place by using the given directions.)

廁所

左邊

公共汽車站
→你

停車場

加油站

公用電話

右邊

你 的 右 邊 是 _____   你 在 哪 兒 ？ _____

出公共汽車站，向左拐，就會看到 ——————

停車場的後面是——————— 加油站的前面是———————

VI. Look at the map and fill in appropriate words for the following instructions.

公用電話在你的 ———————

走出 ——————向——————就會看到廁所。

停車場在加油站———————。加油站在停車場的———————

VII. Oral exercise

A. Read out loud by using the list words to replace the underlined words

我一<u>放學</u>就想去<u>打球</u>。　　　你<u>往左拐</u>就會看到<u>游泳池</u>。
  1. 做功課，游泳　　　　　　 1. 向前走，教師節慶祝
  2. 吃東西，上廁所　　　　　　 活動
  3. 到親戚家，飯館吃飯　　　 2. 往右拐，加油站
                        3. 向左拐，停車場

您別忘了，<u>鎖匙</u>就在<u>前面</u>。
  1. 兒童樂園，後面
  2. 公用電話亭，旁邊
  3. 牌子，你的左邊

B. Make a sentence for each one of the given words:

旁邊 ————————————————————————

左邊
  ————————————————————————

右邊
  ————————————————————————

問路（二）

乘客：請問中國大飯店在哪一站下車？

司機：你在下一站下車，走到十字路口，往右拐，走到第二個紅綠燈，往左拐，過了紅綠燈，中國大飯店就在前面。

乘客：謝謝您，到站的時候麻煩叫我一聲好嗎？

司機：沒問題。您是去那兒吃飯嗎？

乘客：不是，我是到飯店旁邊的一家百貨公司去會一個朋友。

司機：那家是不是叫幸運百貨公司？

乘客：是啊！怎麼回事？

司機：那家原來叫幸運，後來關門了，現在叫健康百貨，已經搬家到別的地方了。

乘客：真的！我的朋友怎麼沒告訴我。他一直在那兒做事。

司機：你如果要去健康百貨公司，在快樂兒童樂園站下，下車後，一直走，走到第二個紅綠燈就可以看到健康百貨公司的牌子在你的右手邊。

乘客：謝謝您，今天真幸運，幸好有你幫我，要不然，我就迷路了。

New words

Intersection	get off a car	the first	traffic light	department store	driver	hotel
十字路口	下車	第一	紅綠燈	百貨公司	司機	飯店
shí zì lù kǒu	xià chē	dì yī	hóng lǜ dēng	bǎi huò gōng sī	sī jī	fàn diàn

Passenger	to move	straight/all the time	to get lost	otherwise	next stop
乘客	搬家	一直	迷路	要不然	下一站
chéng kè	bān jiā	yì zhí	mí lù	yào bù rán	xià yí zhàn

to work	bankrupt	others	originally	to meet friends	what's the matter	fortunately
做事	關門	別的	原來	會朋友	怎麼回事	幸好
zuò shì	guān mén	bié de	yuán lái	huì péng yǒu	zěn me huí shì	xìng hǎo

Something you need to know

Ordinal numbers

For ordinal numbers, Chinese use 第 *di* before the number.

For example:　　　第一 *the first*　　　第二 *the second*　　　第三 *the third*

I.　　Write in English for the following words.

1. 十字路口 _____

2. 一直 _____

3. 飯店 _____

4. 怎麼回事 _____

5. 要不然 _____

6. 迷路 _____

7. 做事 _____

8. 百貨公司 _____

9. 紅綠燈 _____

10. 第一 _____

11. 搬家 _____

12. 乘客 _____

13. 司機 _____

14. 下車 _____

15. 會朋友 _____

16. 下一站 _____

17. 別的 _____

18. 幸好 _____

19. 原來 _____

II. Follow the stroke order and write a complete character in each box.

口口口口
kǒu

第第第第第第第第
dì

怎怎怎怎怎怎
zěn

綠綠綠綠綠綠綠綠綠
lǜ

燈燈燈燈燈燈燈
dēng

貨貨貨貨貨貨
huò

司司司
sī

機機機機機機機機
jī

乘乘乘乘乘乘
chéng

搬搬搬搬搬搬搬
bān

53

原原原原原原原
yuán

然然然然然然
rán

迷 迷 迷 迷 迷 迷
mí

店店店店店店
diàn

III.　Write in Chinese for the following words.

1. Intersection: _____

2. Passenger: _____

3. Otherwise: _____

4. What's the matter: _____

5. Get off the car: _____

6. To move: _____

7. To get lost: _____

8. Traffic light: _____

9. Straight: _____

10. Hotel: _____

11. Originally: _____

12. Department store: _____

13. Work: _____

14. Others: _____

15. To meet friends: _____

16. Bankrupt: _____

IV.　Fill in the blanks according to the chapter context.

你在下一站下車，走到_____，往右拐，走到第一個紅綠燈，往左拐，過了_____，中國大飯店就在前面。到站的時候_____叫我一聲好嗎？

你在下一站＿＿＿＿，走到十字路口，＿＿＿＿＿，看到第一個紅綠燈，＿＿＿＿，過了紅綠燈，中國大飯店就在前面。

＿＿＿＿＿：那家原來叫幸運，後來＿＿＿＿＿了，現在叫健康百貨，已經＿＿＿＿到別的地方了。

V. Translate the following into Chinese.

1. Fortunately I have you to help me, otherwise I could have gotten lost.

2. Get off at next stop (and) go straight until the traffic light.

3. That department store was called lucky, (but) it is bankrupt afterward.

4. Turn right at the second traffic light, and go straight.

5. They have moved to the other place already.

6. The drive goes to a department store to meet the passenger.

I. Look at the map and give the direction

公共汽車　　十字路口　　中國大飯店　　紅綠燈　　百貨公司　　加油站　　紅綠燈　　停車場　　車站

A. If you are a bus driver, how do you tell your passenger where to get off or the direction, if your passenger wants to go to:

中國大飯店： 過了＿＿＿＿＿＿ 在 ＿＿＿＿＿＿＿＿下車。

車站： 走到＿ 二個＿＿＿ 往 ＿＿＿ 車站就在你的＿＿＿

百貨公司：＿＿＿＿＿＿＿＿＿＿＿＿＿＿＿＿＿＿＿＿

B. Look at the same map to locate the places while you reading the questions.

走過十字路口，你會看到中國大飯店在你的右手邊，在第一個
紅綠燈向左拐，就是

＿＿＿＿＿＿＿＿＿＿

過了第二個紅綠燈，一直 走，就是 ＿＿＿＿＿＿＿＿＿

在百貨公司前面的就是 ＿＿＿＿＿＿＿＿＿

從中國大飯店出來，往右拐，一直走，過了第二個紅綠燈就是

＿＿＿＿＿＿＿＿

VII. Oral exercise
Look at the same map and give the directions for the following places.
1. 如果你從飯店出來，要去百貨公司

2. 如果你在百貨公司，要去車站

3. 如果你從車站走路去大飯店

4. 如果你是司機，要去停車場

5. 如果你是司機，要去加油站

買水果

你　：老板，這個西瓜多少錢？

老板：一個一百八十塊錢，兩個三百五。

你　：很便宜，我買兩個。

老板：你今天運氣好，是我的第一個顧客，我便宜賣給你。

你　：謝謝妳，老板。蘋果怎麼賣？

老板：一個十二塊錢，五個五十八塊錢，不甜不要錢。

你　：太貴了，我就買西瓜吧！這是四百塊錢，找我五十塊錢。

老板：對不起，我沒有零錢，要不要再買一些別的？今年的橘子又大又甜，七個算你五十塊錢就好。

你　：好吧！就買七個吧！

老板：你今天運氣好，都買到了便宜貨。

你　：老板，這個橘子壞了。

老板：對不起，您看到這個牌子上寫的字沒有？ **"貨物出門，概不退換"**

57

New words

Overall	return	exchange	merchandise	orange	spoil	melon	water	fortune
概	退	換	貨物	橘子	壞	瓜	水	運氣
gài	tuì	huàn	huò wù	jú zi	huài	guā	shuǐ	yùn qì

Watermelon	fruit	cheap	customer	apple	sweet	to give change	changes
西瓜	水果	便宜	顧客	蘋果	甜	找錢	零錢
xī guā	shuǐ guǒ	pián yí	gù kè	píng guǒ	tián	zhǎo qián	líng qián

Some	these	how	door	to go out the door	boss
一些	這些	怎麼	門	出門	老板
yì xiē	zhè xiē	zěn me	mén	chū mén	lǎo bǎn

Something you need to know

The use of 塊錢 *kuai qian*

Sometimes the word 塊錢 *kuai qian* can be omitted or replaced by the word
元 *yuan*. (see next chapter) For example:

五十塊錢   *fifty dollars*

is the same as 五十元
and is the same as 五十。
*三百五 is the same as 三百五十塊錢。

I.   Write in English for the following words.

dà gài: _____   yì xiē   _____

huò wù   _____   xī guā   _____

tuì huàn   _____   píng guǒ _____

jú zi   zhǎo qián

huài yùn qì _____   líng qián _____

shuǐ guǒ   _____   gù kè   _____

mǎi yī sòng yī _____   pián yí   _____

II. Follow the stroke order and write a complete character in each box.

門門門門門門
mén

概概概概概概概
gài

退退退退退退退退
tuì

換換換換換換換
huàn

水水水水水
shuǐ

橘橘橘橘橘橘橘橘
jú

壞壞壞壞壞壞壞壞
huài

瓜瓜瓜瓜瓜
guā

便便便便便便便
pián

宜宜宜宜宜宜
yí

蘋蘋蘋蘋蘋蘋蘋
píng

甜甜甜甜甜甜
tián

零零零零零零零零
líng

些些些些些些些
xiē

板板板板板板
bǎn

III. Write in Chinese for the following words.

1. Overall: _____

2. Return or exchange: _____ _____

3. Spoil: _____

4. Orange: _____ _____

5. Merchandise: _____ _____

6. Watermelon: _____ _____

7. Cheap: _____ _____

8. Fortune: _____ _____

9. Customer: _____ _____

10. Apple: _____ _____

11. Sweet: _____

12. Changes: _____ _____

13. Some: _____ _____

14. Go out the door: _____ _____

IV. Fill in the blanks according to the context.

_____ ，這個西瓜多少錢？

很 _____ ，我買兩個。

你今天運氣好，是我的第一個 _____ 。

對不起，我沒有零錢，要不要再買＿＿＿＿別的？

你看到這牌子上寫的字沒有？"＿＿＿＿＿＿＿＿＿＿＿＿"

老板，這個＿＿＿＿壞了。

老板，＿＿＿＿怎麼賣？

老板，這個橘子＿＿＿＿。

這是四百塊錢，＿＿＿＿我五十塊錢。

V. Translate the following into Chinese.

1. These apples and oranges are all spoiled.

2. They cannot be returned or exchanged, (if) the merchandise is out of the door.

3. This sign writes "no sweet no money". (Don't want money if it's not sweet.)

				著	"					"

4. Boss, how much is the watermelon?

5. You are the first customer, I'll sell to you cheap.

		一			我				

6. Watermelon is very sweet, just 50 dollars for you.

				你				就	好

VI. **What do you say under the following situation? (Write your response in Chinese.)**

1. You want to know how much the orange is._____

_____

2. Tell your customers these apples and watermelons are very sweet.

_____

3. If these fruits are not sweet, you don't need to pay anything.

_____

4. You sell oranges very cheap to your first customer and you want him to know about it.

_____

5. You give the boss one hundred Taiwan dollars and ask him to give you fifty dollars change back.

_____

6. You don't have change, so tell your customer to buy something else.

_____

VII. **Oral exercise**

Draw one watermelon, five apples, and seven oranges.
Set the prices for them according to the chapter context and sell them to an adult.

買衣服

店主：買一送一，大減價，大拍賣。

顧客一：小姐，那件綠色毛衣多少錢？

店主：買一送一，買就送，兩百九十九元，送一件粉紅色內衣。

顧客二：我想買一件橘紅色短裙和一件白色短褲。

店主：這件褲裙打八折，你要不要？

顧客二：打完折多少錢？

店主：算你五百九十九塊九毛九吧！

顧客二：什麼！這麼貴！

短裙

店主：這是最新美國進口的，最流行的樣式。

顧客二：我剛從美國回來，怎麼沒看過這個樣式的衣服？

店主：這樣好了，我再打對折給你，算你好運，只賣給你三百塊就好。

顧客二：算了，不買了，這個店主不老實。

店主：喂！小姐你別走，算你兩百九十九塊九毛九，再送一件上衣。

顧客二：我們還是到不二價商店去吧！

短褲

New words

Store owner	store	dollar	import	pink color	buy one get one free	on sale	a dime
店主	商店	元	進口	粉紅色	買一送一	拍賣	毛
diàn zhǔ	shāng diàn	yuán	jìn kǒu	fēn hóng sè	mǎi yī sòng yī	pāi mài	máo

Shorts	reduced price	skirt	honest	underwear	style	sweater	never mind
短褲	減價	裙子	老實	內衣	樣式	毛衣	算了
duǎn kù	jiǎn jià	qún zi	lǎo shí	nèi yī	yàng shì	máo yī	suàn le

clothes	no bargain	discount	50% off	orange color	20% off	top
衣服	不二價	打折	打對折	橘紅色	打八折	上衣
yī fú	bú èr jià	dǎ zhé	dǎ duì zhé	jú hóng sè	dǎ bā zhé	shàng yī

I.   Write in English for the following words.

1. diàn zhǔ : _____

2. shāng diàn: _____

3. lǎo shí : _____

4. bú èr jià: _____

5. yuán: _____

6. jìn kǒu: _____

7. mǎi yī sòng yī: _____

8. pāi mài: _____

9. fēn hóng sè : _____

10. jiǎn jià: _____

11. suàn le: _____

12. yàng shì: _____

13. nèi yī : _____

14. máo yī : _____

15. duǎn kù : _____

16. qún zi: _____

17. yī fú : _____

18. dǎ duì zhé: _____

20. jú hóng sè: _____

21. dǎ bā zhé: _____

22. shàng yī: _____

22. liǎng máo wǔ _____

I. Follow the stroke order and write a complete character in each box.

衣衣衣衣衣衣
yī

服服服服服
fú

件件件件
jiàn

減減減減減減減減
jiǎn

價價價價價價價
jià

拍拍拍拍拍
pāi

元元元元
yuán

內內內內內
nèi

粉粉粉粉粉粉粉
fēn

褲褲褲褲褲褲褲褲褲
kù

裙裙裙裙裙裙裙
qún

實 實 實 實 實 實 實 實 實

shí

商 商 商 商 商 商

shāng

進 進 進 進 進 進 進

jìn

折 折 折 折

zhé

II. Write in Chinese for the following words.

1. Store owner: _____ _____

2. Reduced price: _____ _____

3. Clothes: —— ——

4. Buy one get one free:__ ___ ___ ——

5. Sweater: —— ——

6. Pink color: ___ ___ ____

7. Orange color: —— —— ——

8. On sale: _____ _____

9. Dollar: ——

10. Underwear: ____ ____

11. No bargain: _____ _____ _____

12. Store: _____ _____

13. Honest: —— ——

14. Import: _____ _____

15. 20% off: ____ ____ ____

16. 50% off: ____ ____ ____

17. Never mind: —— ——

18. Style: _____ _____

19. Shorts: ____ ____

20. Skirt: _____ ____

III. Fill in the blanks according to the chapter context.

買一送一，人 _____ ，大 _____ 。

買就送，買兩百九十九元，送一件 _____ 。

我想買一件 _____ 色 _____ 和一件白色 _____ 。

這是最新美國 _____ 的最 _____ _____ 。

我再打 _____ 給你，算你好運。

_____ ，不買了，這個店主不 _____

我們還是到不 _____ 去吧。

IV. Translate the following into Chinese.

Buy one get one free, reduced price, on sale.

I want to buy an orange shorts.

This newly imported (merchandise) from the United States that is the most popular (fashion) style.

I'll give 50% off again (more).

Miss, how much is that green sweater?

Never mind, let's go to the no bargain store.

V. Answer the questions according to your real situation.

1. 你都是和誰一起去買衣服？_____

2. 你有綠色或是紅色的上衣嗎？_____

3. 你喜歡到小商店還是大百貨公司去買東西？_____

4. 橘紅色和粉紅色，你喜歡哪一個？_____

5. 一百塊錢打八折後是多少錢？_____

6. 一千元打對折是多少錢？_____

7. 西瓜、蘋果和橘子，你喜歡哪一樣水果？_____

8. 通常你的長褲、上衣、內衣哪一件貴？_____

9. 媽媽的裙子便宜，還是爸爸的褲子？_____

10.貨物價錢不變的商店是什麼商店？_____

VI. Oral exercise

You are a salesperson; you have the merchandise for sale as indicated below:

裙子 $120   長褲 $200   短褲 $80   內衣 $69.99   上衣 $255

Sell these clothes to an adult with some discounts. For example:
20% off for the skirt, 50% off for the long pants…….

You can also set up your own price and either use American dollars or Taiwan dollars.

Wrap up

I.   Fill in the blanks with appropriate words from the word bank.

> 阿姨，表姐，馬上，麻煩，有空，幫忙，考試，知道，台幣
> ，車站，電話亭，單程票，乘客，司機，塊錢，售票亭，
> 健康，寄信，點鐘，慶祝，廁所，衣服，商店，大拍賣

1. 媽媽的姐妹，你叫她們 ＿＿＿＿＿＿

2. 媽媽的姐妹生的小孩，如果是女生又比你大，你叫她 ＿＿＿＿＿

3. 通常 ＿＿＿＿＿ 的東西都會比較便宜。

4. 去看電影，你要先到哪兒買票 ＿＿＿＿＿＿＿

5. 表哥，我想 ＿＿＿＿＿ 您教我數學好嗎？

6. 你什麼時候 ＿＿＿＿＿ 到我家來玩？

7. 媽媽在叫你，你最好 ＿＿＿＿＿過去看看。

8. 我希望我們大家都很 ＿＿＿＿＿、快樂。

9. 廁所的鎖匙不見了，請大家 ＿＿＿＿＿ 找找看

10. 這件綠色 ＿＿＿＿＿比那件紅色褲子好看。

11. 奶奶已經下車，在 ＿＿＿＿＿等我們了。

12. 下個月學校要 ＿＿＿＿＿，所以比較忙。

13. 這兒的＿＿＿＿＿都關門了，不知道搬到哪兒去了？

14. 你在這兒等一會兒，她去幫我＿＿＿＿＿馬上回來。

15. 從公用 ＿＿＿＿＿打長途電話太貴了。

16. 對不起，請問車站有沒有＿＿＿＿＿？

17. 公共汽車上幫我們開車的人叫 _____

18. 司機，請將所有_____ 都送到北京大飯店。

19. 美國人用的錢叫美金，台灣人用的錢叫_____

20. 台幣三十三 _____ ，差不多可以買美金一塊錢的東西。

21. 他是這家百貨公司的老板，可是_____的人不多。

22. 每年的十月十日國慶日，我們都回台灣參加 _____ 活動。

23. 火車_____ 當然比雙程票便宜。

24. 直達車上午準時九_____ 出發。

II. Write the appropriate measure words for the phrases whenever it is necessary. *(some of them might not need the measure word)*

Measure words: 件，個，塊，張，本，枝，隻，雙

1. 一 ____ 月

2. 兩 ____ 紙

3. 三 ____ 書

4. 四 ____ 錢

5. 五 ____ 小狗

6. 六 ____ 衣服

7. 七 ____ 鉛筆

8. 八 ____ 頭

9. 九 ____ 手

10. 十 ____ 票

11. 下 ____ 星期

12. 昨 ____ 天

13. 十一 ____ 毛衣

14. 明 ____ 年

15. 十二 ____ 蘋果

16. 十三 ____ 乘客

17. 十四 ____ 腳

18. 十五 ____ 日記

19. 十六 ____ 貓

20. 十七 ____ 牌子

III. Look at the map and answer the questions.

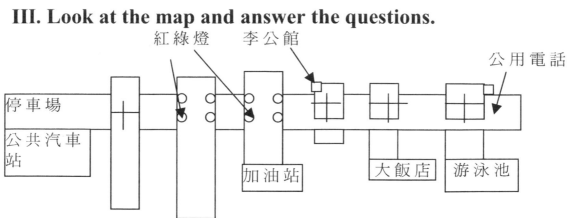

紅綠燈　李公館　　　公用電話

停車場
公共汽車站
加油站
大飯店　游泳池

A. Give each instruction a correct destination. *(Write the destination in the provided space).*

_____　從停車場走到第二個紅綠燈，往右拐，就看到了。

_____　從加油站走出來，在紅綠燈上往左拐，走過第二個紅綠燈以後，下一個十字路口一直走，前面就是停車場，在停車場左邊就是了。

_____　從李公館走到十字路口，向左拐，再走兩個十字路口，在這個十字路口往右拐，一直走，就會看到了。

_____　從大飯店出來，走到路口往右拐，在第二個路口的左前方。

B. Give an appropriate instruction for each destination.

From bus station to Li's resident: _____

_____

Form hotel to parking lot: _____

_____

From swimming pool to Li's resident: _____

_____

From public telephone to gas station: _____

_____

IV. If you go to a big city, you will see all kinds of signs. Following are some signs you might see in the city, can you tell what are those signs mean? *(Write in English)*

買一送一		公用電話亭

_____   _____

北京大飯店		公共汽車站

_____   _____

男廁所	李公館	台南大百貨公司

_____ _____ _____

對折大拍賣		最新流行衣服減價商店

_____   _____

台北火車站		特甜水果，不甜不要錢

_____   _____

游泳池	加油站	售票亭

_____ _____

貨物出門，概不退換		電腦減價大拍賣

_____   _____

V. Look at the pictures and write their names in Chinese

_____   _____   _____

_____   _____   _____

_____   _____   _____

_____

73

I.   **Write a letter to your grandma and tell her:**

        a.   **You have received the gift she sent to you**
        b.   **How you celebrated your birthday**
        c.   **Where you went to celebrate your birthday**
        d.   **You wish your grandma happy and healthy**

_____ :

_____

_____

_____

_____

_____

_____

_____

                                                _____

                                                _____

VII. Complete the statements by using the words given:

李： 麻煩您幫我寄信好嗎？

王：_____ (No problem)我現在就去，_____回來。 (at once)

李： 謝謝您！

王：_____。 (you are welcome)

° °

張： _____ 是謝 _____？ (Is this xie resident? Use polite form)

人： _____ (No, you had the wrong number.)

張：_____ (Sorry!)

° 顧

客： _____ (I would like to buy some apples.)

老板：_____
_____ (80% off if you buy 10 apples.)

林小姐：_____
_____ (How much is it to make a long distance call to Taiwan?)

林先生： _____
_____ (It is very expensive to use the public phone to call long distance.)

° °

售票員： _____. (The one way ticket is cheaper.)

乘客： ——————————. (What time the express train arrives?)

售票員：—————————— (Noon twelve o'clock sharp.)

乘客：—————————— (What time is it now?)

售票員： _____
_____ (It is 9:25 now, but the train departs at 9:30.)

VIII. Oral exercise

A. Create a phone conversation with an adult or your friend.
"Your aunt is calling your mom, but she just went out to mail a letter. You write down aunt's phone number and will tell mother to return her call, as soon as she gets home."

B. Make up a dialog with a friend or an adult that includes the following information.
"You are going to see a relative in Tainan. She is coming to pick you up at 9:30P.M. but you don't know whether to take express train or regular train. You need suggestions from the ticket seller, and also the price difference."

C. Practice the conversation between a storeowner and a customer.
"You are a customer who want to buy some fruits and clothes. What you would buy depends on the price, but you want to buy at least three things. Of course, if the price is lower the better chance you would buy it."

(Translation)   ## Buying Tickets

Li: Sir, I would like to buy a train ticket to Tainan.
Ticket seller: Miss, do you want the regular train ticket or express train ticket?
Li: What is the difference?
Ticket seller: The regular train will stop at every station, but the express train goes straight to Tainan without making stops in the middle. The express train is much faster than the regular train.
Li: How much is a express train ticket?
Ticket seller: A one-way ticket is four hundred and fifty dollars.
Li: What about the regular train? How much each?
Ticket seller: For the regular train, a one-way ticket is two hundred and twenty a piece, and two-way tickets, or round trip tickets are four hundred and forty dollar each.
Li: OK! I'll buy a regular train round trip ticket.
Li: May I ask, What time does the train leave? When will it arrive at Tainan?
Ticket seller: The train schedule is outside the ticket booth. You can go to see it yourself.
Li: Thank you.
Ticket seller: You are welcome.

A Letter to Grandma

Dear Grandma:

How are you? I am fine!
I have received the gift you sent to me, thank you!

Yesterday, Father took us to the South. Early in the morning, we arrived at the train station, and bought four express train one-way tickets. Notlong after that, the train arrived.

We were originally going to buy round trip tickets, but because of the holiday, all the tickets were sold out, so we had to buy the returning tickets from Tainan after we arrived there.

The express train arrived Tainan very soon. Once we got off the train, Father immediately went to the ticket booth to buy the tickets. As a result, he could only buy the regular train tickets, moreover, the returning tickets were more expensive. They were fifty dollars more than what we had spent on the coming tickets. However, the ticket seller said that it was not bad to be able to get a ticket during the holidays.

Grandma, I really wished you could have gone with us to Tainan. Younger brother and I are missing you very much. When will you come to see us?
                         To wish respectfully
Grandma healthy and happiness

                                        Your Grandchild
                                        Guo-Sheng
                                        Presented respectfully

My Diary

9/28/1999   *Tuesday, Weather: no rain*

Today is a special day because today is Mother's birthday and Teacher's Day, too. Mother said that every year at this day, all the schools in Taiwan have a day off. Mother is a teacher, so she has a day off, too. Her friends will invite her to the movies to celebrate her birthday. Mother said that Teacher's Day is to remember the greatest teacher---Confucius. Usually there are activities to celebrate and to remember this great person in Taiwan, every year on this day.

We asked Mother what present she would hope us to give her. Mother said, "As long as you are healthy and happy every day and are good childran, it would be the best present for me."

In the evening, Father took us out to eat in a Chinese restaurant. After dinner, the fortune cookie label Mother got was written "Wish you a happy birthday".

Times

Mr.: Miss, may I ask what time it is now?
Miss: Five thirty. It's exactly the time when people get out of work and it's the busiest hour on the road.

Mr. : No wonder the number six bus is not here yet.
Miss: The number six bus has stopped running lately. Don't you know that?

Mr. : I didn't know, because I just came to Taiwan from the U. S. A. last month.
Miss: No wonder. The newest bus schedule is outside of the station. I'll take you there to see it.

Mr. : I am going to Taichung to see relatives and I'm planning to come back tomorrow afternoon. Which bus do you think I should take?
Miss: There is one at five-forty, one at six o'clock, and there is another one at six-o-five to Taichung, too.

Mr. :If I take this express bus at six sharp, how long will it take to get from here to Taichung?
Miss : Maybe two hours. If your departure is on time at six o'clock sharp, you will arrive at eight. When you come back tomorrow, you can take the bus at twelve sharp in noon to Taipei. You will arrive exactly two o'clock in the afternoon.

Mr. : Wonderful! Thank you!
Miss: You are welcome!

Ask for the direction (I)

You: Excuse me, where is the restroom?

He: When you walk out the station and turn right, you will see the sign hanging outside the restroom. When you see it you will know.

You: Is there a public phone booth next to the restroom?

He: Yes! The restroom is at the left of the public phone booth.

You: I remember that the gas station is in front of the restroom. Is it right?

He: Yes! There is a parking lot in the back. Don't forget to get the key from the gas station people.

You: I almost forgot. Thank you.

He: You are welcome.

Ask for the direction (II)

Passenger: Excuse me, which stop should I get off to the China Grand Hotel?
Driver: When you get off at the next stop, walk to the intersection, turn right, walk to the first traffic light, turn left, and pass the traffic light, the China Grand Hotel is right in front of you.

Passenger: Thank you, will you call me when we get to the stop?
Driver: No problem. Are you going to eat there?

Passenger: No, I am going to meet a friend in a department store beside the restaurant.
Driver: Is that the one called Luck Department Store?

Passenger: Yes! What is the matter?
Driver: It was originally called Luck but bankrupted later on, and it's called Healthy Department Store now, but has moved to other place.

Passenger: Really? Why didn't my friend tell me? He works there all the time.
Driver: If you are going to the Healthy Department Store, you get off at the Happy Children's Amusement Park. After you get off the bus, go straight, walk to the second traffic light, and you will see the Healthy Department Store sign to your right hand side.

Passenger: Thank you, I am very lucky today. Fortunately, I have you to help me, otherwise I might have gotten lost.

Buying Fruits

You: Boss, how much is this watermelon?
Boss: A hundred eighty each, two for three hundred fifty.

You: It's very cheap. I'll buy two.
Boss: You are lucky today. You are my first customer so I will sell them to you cheap.

You: Thank you, boss. How do you sell the apples?
Boss: Twelve dollars each, five for fifty-eight dollars. You don't need to pay me, if they are not sweet.

You: Too expensive, I'll just buy the watermelon. Here are four hundred dollars, give me fifty dollars in change.
Boss: Sorry, I don't have change. Do you want to buy something else?
This year's oranges are big and sweet, seven for fifty dollars just for you.

You: OK! I'll buy seven.
Boss: You are lucky today. You got all the cheap prices.

You: Boss, this orange is spoiled.

Boss: Sorry, did you see what was written on the sign? "No merchandise is returned or exchanged, if it has gone out of the door"

Buying Clothes

Storeowner: Buy one get one free, big reduced price, big sale!
Customer 1: Miss, how much is that green sweater?
Storeowner: Buy one get one free, you buy and we give. Two hundred ninety-nine dollars, and we will give you pink underwear for free.

Customer 2: I would like to buy an orange short skirt and a white shorts.
Storeowner: This short-skirt is 20% off, do you want it?

Customer 2: How much is it after the discount?
Storeowner: It's five hundred ninety-nine dollars and ninety-nine cents just for you.

Customer 2: What? So expensive!
Storeowner: This has been newly imported from the U. S. A. It is the most popular style.

Customer 2: I just returned from the U. S. A., why haven't I ever seen these clothes in this kind of style?
Storeowner: How about this, I'll give you another 50% off. You are lucky, I'll sell to you for only three hundred dollars.

Customer: Never mind! I don't want to buy it. This storeowner is not honest.
Storeowner: Hey! Miss, don't go, I'll give you two hundred ninety-nine dollars and ninety-nine cents and a top for free.Customer 2: Let's go to the no bargain store

(Page 4 ~ 12)
I.
1. female cousin
2. To bother
3. No problem
4. Aunt
5. To inform
6. To joke
7. To tell
8. You're welcome
9. Test
10. At once
II.
1. J 2. H 3. K
4. C 5. R 6. E
7. G 8. P 9. Q
10. A 11. M 12. B
13. O 14. F 15. D
16. I 17. N 18. L
III.
1阿姨 2公館
3表姐 4通知
5剛到 6記下
7馬上 8不客氣
林阿姨
對不起我打錯
電話了
喂，請問這兒是
林公館嗎
表姐
先通知一聲
剛到
剛剛才出去
電話幾號
記下來了
馬上
謝謝
不客氣
(Page 9)
1麻煩 2有空
3告訴 4多久
5知道 6幫我
7補 8問題

9鐘頭 10多少錢
11開玩笑
12幫我 13考試

麻煩，空
先告訴
知道，幫我補
沒問題，
鐘頭多少錢
跟你開玩笑
考完試再謝
我吧
IV
1喂，請問是林
公館嗎
2是啊！你找哪位
3你什麼時候來
美國的，怎麼不
先通知一聲
4剛到沒幾天，
我過幾天來看您
5請等一下，我去
看看她在不在
6表姐剛剛才出去
等一下她一回來
我馬上叫她打電
話給你
7你的電話幾號
8不客氣，姨媽
9我有事想麻煩您
明天您有沒有空
10你先告訴我什
麼事，你知道我
才來美國沒多久
11我想請你幫我
補數學
12沒問題，一個
鐘頭多少錢
13跟你開玩笑的
V
你打錯電話了

2請等一下，我去
看看她在不在
3爸爸剛剛才出去
他一回來我馬上
叫他打電話給你
4不客氣
5我有事想麻煩你
6請問林伯伯電話
幾號
7我想請你幫我
補數學
8沒問題，一個
鐘頭多少錢
9等一下再謝我
VI
請問是林公館嗎
對不起，你打錯
電話了
你的電話是不是
3456789
是啊，可是這兒
不是林公館
林小姐在嗎
我是，請問你是
哪位
表姐，這是小龍
小龍，你什麼時
候來美國的
剛到沒幾天
為什麼不先通知
一聲
我不想麻煩你
星期三晚上你
有沒有空？我想來
看你
好，我來接你，
你住在哪兒？
先告訴我你在
這兒做什麼
我在幫一個女生
補英文

好，一個鐘頭多
少錢
跟你開玩笑的
(Page 16～21)
1. J 2. Q 3. P
4. B 5. R 6. C
7. L 8. M 9. D
10. N 11. G 12. H
13. I 14. E 15. A
16. F 17. O 18. K
III.
1先生 2小姐
3公共汽車
4車站 5公用
電話 6表哥
7外面 8也許
9太貴了
10五塊錢
11美金 12台幣
13放心 14本地
15長途 16國王
17貴姓 18記得
IV
1先生
2記得
3公共汽車
4貴姓
5國王
6表哥
7車站
8太貴了
9本地
10也許
11五塊錢，台幣
12長途電話
VI
先生請問哪兒有
公用電話
2我記得這附近有
一個公共汽車站
3她用公用電話打
長途電話

4小姐請問您貴姓
5英國國王不會打
長途電話
6這張電影票太貴
了
7公共汽車票多少
錢
8放心是台幣不是
美金

(Page 23~27)
I.
　　1. F 2. G 3. J
　　4. I 5. H 6. A
　　7. B 8. E 9. D
　　10. C 11. M
　　12. L 13. K

III.
1買 2火車票
3售票員
4普通車 5直達車
6單程 7雙程
8時間表 9售票亭
10中間 11兩百
塊錢 12台南
IV
1台北，台南
2售票亭
3售票員
4直達車、普通車
5單程
6雙程
7直達車票
8中間
9時間表，外面
10停
V
1雙程火車票一張
多少錢
2請問售票亭在
哪兒

3請問售票員是
哪位
4火車時間表在
哪兒
5普通車和直達
車有什麼不一樣
6直達車比較快
7普通車中間會停
8火車票兩百三十
五塊錢台幣
VI
1從台北到台南要
多久
2普通車什麼時候
到台中
3直達車比較快可
是比較貴
4售票員就站在售
票亭外面
5單程火車票一張
兩百七十九塊錢
6時間表在外面你
可以自己去看
(Page 29～33)
I
1P 2B 3L 4Q 5D 6E
7M 8G 9A 10O 11R 12J
13K 14N 15F 16I
17 H 18 C
III
1健康　　2寄信
3所有的　　4期間
5不錯　　6敬上
7想念　　8親愛
9賣光　　10到達
11假日　　12關係
13回程票　14結果
15孫　　16快樂
17本來　　18敬祝
IV
1親愛　　2想念

V
1親愛的表姐我們都很想念您
2爺爺您寄來的禮物我們都收到了
3一大早我們就到達火車站
4他想買直達車票給你
5因為假日關係所有的票都賣光了
6我們在售票亭買了回程票
7結果我們只買兩張普通車票
8敬祝您健康快樂

(Page 35~39)
I
1C 2B 3J 4F 5I 6M
7L 8E 9N 10G 11A
12D 13K 14O 15H
III
1吃飯　　2飯館
3特別　　4通常
5慶祝　　6日記
7教師節　8人物
9紀念　　10孔子
11放假　　12晴
13幸運簽　14偉大
15活動
IV
1日記　　2晴
3飯館　　4吃飯
5特別　　6教師節
7放假　　8活動
9偉大　　10人物
11孔子　　12幸運簽
13紀念　　14通常
15慶祝
V
1今天是特別的日子所以學校放假
2教師節爸爸帶我們去飯館吃飯
3爺爺是一個偉大的人物
4我通常每天寫日記
5孔子的生日台灣有很多慶祝活動
6幸運簽告訴我我的考試沒問題

(Page 41 ~ 45)
I
1早上五點半
2下午六點四十五分
3中午十二點整
4早上三點五分
5早上十二點五十五分
6下午兩點五十分
III
1一半　　2正是
3難怪　　4怪不得
5時刻表　6出發
7親戚　　8打算
9下午　　10如果
11搭　　12準時
13剛好　14往
15公車　16忙
IV
1請問現在幾點鐘
2正是下班時間路上最忙的時候
3你打算什麼時候出發
4如果公車準時出發我們中午會到
5剛好十二點整
6難怪我的親戚這麼忙
7車站外面有新的時刻表
8怪不得你要搭普通車
VI
1現在是中國時間下午六點半
2難怪時刻表沒有六路車
3十點半有一班十一點整也有一班中午十二點還有一班
4也許兩個鐘頭也許兩個半鐘頭

(Page 48 ~ 50)
II
1廁所　　2旁邊
3右拐　　4左拐
5牌子　　6加油站
7停車場　8鎖匙
9差點　　10別忘了
11後面　12前面
III
廁所，牌子
旁邊，左邊
前面，加油站
後面，停車場
鎖匙，差點
IV
1走出公車站外面往左拐

2公用電話亭就在左邊
3加油站在前面
停車場在後面
4廁所的鎖匙就在你的右邊
5我差點忘了旁邊有一個牌子
V
公用電話亭，公共汽車站
廁所
加油站，停車場
VI
右邊
公共汽車站
左拐
前面，後面

(Page 52～56)
I
1. Intersection
2. Straight
3. Hotel
4. What's the matter
5. Otherwise
6. Get lost
7. Work
8. Department store
9. Traffic light
10. The first
11. to move
12. Passenger
13. Driver
14. Get off a car
15. To meet friends
16. Next stop
17. Others
18. Originally
II
1十字路口
2乘客　3要不然
4怎麼回事

5下車　6搬家
7迷路　8紅綠燈
9一直　10飯店
11原來
12百貨公司
13做事　14別的
15會朋友　16關門
III
十字路口，紅綠燈
麻煩，下車，右拐
往左拐，司機，關門，搬家
IV
1幸好有你幫我要不然我就迷路了
2在下一站下車一直走到紅綠燈
3那家百貨公司原來叫幸運後來關門了
4第二個紅綠燈向右拐一直走
5他們已經搬到別的地方了
6司機去百貨公司會乘客
V
A十字路口，中國大飯店站，第，紅綠燈，右拐，左邊，走到第一個紅綠燈往左拐
B百貨公司
停車場
加油站
停車場

(Page 58～62)

I.
1. overall
2. merchandise
3. return & exchange
4. orange
5. bad fortune
6. fruit
7. buy one get one free
8. some
9. watermelon
10. apple
11. give change
12. changes
13. customer
14. cheap
III.
1概　　2退換
3壞　　4橘子
5貨物　6西瓜
7便宜　8運氣
9顧客　10蘋果
11甜　　12零錢
13一些　14出門
15買一送一
IV
老板，便宜
顧客，一些
貨物出門概不退換
橘子，蘋果
壞了，找
V
1這些蘋果和橘子都壞了
2貨物出門概不退換
3這個牌子寫著不甜不要錢
4老板西瓜多少錢
5你是第一個顧客我便宜賣給你

6西瓜很甜算你五
十塊錢就好
VI
1橘子怎麼賣
2這些蘋果和西瓜
都很甜
3不甜不要錢
4你是第一個顧客
便宜賣給你
5這是一百塊錢請
找我五十塊錢
6我沒有零錢要不
要再買一些別的

(Page 64 ~ 68)
I.
1. Store owner
2. Store
3. Honest
4. No bargain
5. Dollar
6. Import
7. Buy one get one free
8. On sale
9. Pink color
10. Reduced price
11. Never mind
12. Style
13. Underwear
14. Sweater
15. Shorts
16. Skirt
17. Clothes
18. 50% off
19. Orange color
20. 20% off
21. Top
22. Twenty five cents
III
1店主　　2減價
3衣服　　4上衣
5毛衣　　6粉紅色
7橘紅色 8拍賣
9元　　　10內衣

11不二價 12商店
13老實　　14進口
15打八折 16打對折
17算了　　18樣式
19短褲　　20裙子
IV
減價，拍賣
粉紅色內衣
橘紅，短裙，短褲
進口，流行，樣式
對折，算了，老實
二價商店
V
買一送一大減價
大拍賣
我要買一件橘紅色
短褲
這是最新美國進口
的最流行樣式
我再打對折給你
小姐那件綠色毛衣
多少錢
算了我們到不二價
商店去

(Wrap up)
I.
1阿姨　　2表姐
3大拍賣 4售票亭
5麻煩　　6有空
7馬上　　8健康
9幫忙　　10衣服
11車站　　12考試
13商店　　14寄信
15電話　　16廁所
17司機　　18乘客
19台幣　　20塊錢
21知道　　22慶祝
23單程票 24點鐘
II
1個 2張 3本 4塊

5隻 6件 7枝 8個
9雙 10張 11個 12-
13件 14 - 15個
16名 17隻 18本
19隻 20塊
III

A
加油站
公共汽車站
游泳池
公用電話
B
在停車場往前走
，過了第二個紅
綠燈在下一個路
口往左拐就是了

從大飯店走到路
口，往左拐一直
走過了第二個紅
綠燈下一個路口
前面

走到路口往左拐
在第二個路口往
右李公館就在左
前方

一直走到第一個
紅綠燈往左拐加
油站就在前面

IV.

Buy one get one free		Public phone
Beijing grand hotel		Bus stop
Men's room	Li's resident	Tainan Department Store
50% off on sale		Fastion clothes discount store
Taipei Train Station	Sweet Fruits, if they're not sweet you'll get money back	
Swimming pool	Gass Station	Ticket booth
There is no rcturn or exchange after the sale.	Computer on sale	

鎖匙　　　電話　　　裙子
褲子　　　上衣　　　飯
西瓜　　　橘子　　　蘋果
台幣（一百元）

VII

沒問題，馬上　　　　　　　用公用電話打長途電話很貴
不客氣　　　　　　　　　　單程票比較便宜
請問，謝公館嗎　　　　　　直達車什麼時候到達
不是，你打錯電話了　　　　中午十二點整
對不起　　　　　　　　　　現在幾點鐘
我想買一些蘋果　　　　　　現在是九點二十五分，可是
打兩折，如果你買十個蘋果　火車九點半開
打長途電話到台灣多少錢

第四冊生字拼音索引
Pinyin Index
(Entry numbers are given after each item)

第四冊生字、生詞英文索引
Index to new words and phrases